Lead & Succe

Do-More-With-L

6 Shortcuts to

Employee
Engagement

Vicki Hess, RN

6 Shortcuts to

Employee Engagement

Lead & Succeed in a
Do-More-With-Less World

Healthcare Edition

www.**6ShortcutsToEngagement**.com/BonusTools

Inquiries regarding permission for use of the material contained in this book should be addressed to:

Catalyst Consulting, LLC
9 Pinewood Farm Court
Owings, MD 21117

Printed in the United States of America
ISBN: 978-0-9789862-6-1

Credits
Collaborative Editor

Juli Baldwin, The Baldwin Group, Plano, TX
Juli@BaldwinGrp.com

Copy Editor
Design, art direction, and production

Kathleen Green, The Baldwin Group, Plano, TX
Melissa Cabana, Back Porch Creative, Plano, TX
info@BackPorchCreative.com

Other Books by Vicki Hess, RN, MS, Certified Speaking Professional

SHIFT to Professional Paradise: 5 Steps to Less Stress, More Energy & Remarkable Results at Work

The Nurse Manager's Guide to Hiring, Firing & Inspiring

The 28-Day Professional Paradise Diary

Dedication

This book is dedicated with awe and respect to individuals everywhere who work in healthcare and continually give of themselves to serve others. I'm so grateful for each of you.

I'm also grateful for Josh & Brian Hess, who supply endless joy in my life.

And to Alan Hess, who is right beside me supporting and loving me every day as we create Personal and Professional Paradise together.

Contents

Are You Winning the
Do-More-With-Less Battle?

Are you exceeding your productivity measures, knocking the socks off patient satisfaction surveys and meeting all of your departmental goals?

Are your employees just as excited to come *to* work as they are to leave?

Is the current level of work you're asking of your team sustainable?

If you answered, "Yes," then congratulations are in order! You are winning the do-more-with-less battle while keeping your employees motivated and energized. Feel free to put this book down and work on an important project that needs your attention. *(And please take a minute to send me an email at vicki@vickihess.com with your success strategies…I'd love to hear what's working!)*

If you said, "No," don't feel discouraged. You – along with thousands of other dedicated and caring healthcare leaders – are extremely busy juggling multiple priorities and managing constant challenges. And if you're anything like the healthcare leaders I talk with regularly, you're also dealing with the "perfect storm" of healthcare reform, economic uncertainty and rapid and continual change – a storm that continues to grow. Take a minute to check off the following challenges that you, your team and your organization are experiencing:

- ❑ Financial cutbacks
- ❑ Healthcare reform uncertainties
- ❑ Reimbursement issues
- ❑ Baby Boomers retiring en masse
- ❑ Mergers and closings
- ❑ Blending multigenerational workers
- ❑ New PI/QI processes
- ❑ Changing models of care
- ❑ Stressed & burned-out leaders
- ❑ Technology changes
- ❑ Restructuring & layoffs
- ❑ Union activity
- ❑ ICD-10 implementation
- ❑ Doing more with less

Most leaders check off at least 10! It's no wonder so many healthcare leaders and employees feel tired, unmotivated and powerless. Unfortunately, the harsh reality is that these challenges are not going away anytime soon.

But there is good news: **The challenges you're facing can be improved through optimized employee engagement.**

Yes, you read that correctly. Engaged employees equip organizations with the fuel to move forward *in spite of* challenges like these. In fact, a report recently released by Towers Watson stated: "Amid the complex business challenges facing hospitals today…workforce issues can all too easily drop in importance on management's agenda. Yet Towers Watson research and practical experience indicate this is precisely the wrong time to take your eye off creating the right employee experience…. The fact is, employees' attitudes and behavior have a direct and material impact on key patient and clinical results, and can be an essential element in effectively adapting to change."[i]

The evidence indicates that **increased employee engagement drives improved patient satisfaction, quality, safety,**

productivity and efficiency, as well as virtually every other metric that we track in healthcare. When team members are actively engaged, it's the equivalent of adding staff without the additional cost! (Have I got your attention now?) Everything ties back to engagement because, ultimately, it always comes down to how well people do their job and how willing they are to do so with passion, energy and effort over time.

The issue of employee engagement is certainly not new. Yet recent statistics show that 60 percent to 70 percent of healthcare employees are either moderately or actively disengaged. Please take a moment to stop and digest that statistic. That's almost three out of every four employees in healthcare who are not actively engaged at work. That's staggering if you really think about it. Doesn't it make you wonder about the effects of all that disengagement on patient care, safety, quality, finances, etc.?

In conducting research for this book, I asked several hospital CEOs why more healthcare organizations aren't adequately addressing employee disengagement with strategies used at highly successful non-healthcare companies. One wise physician CEO summed it up like this: "I think many of us want to, but we don't for a number of reasons: We don't have the will or the know-how. We can't overcome existing organizational culture and inertia. And the tyranny of urgent crises and priorities make engagement issues less visible."

Those sentiments are echoed by healthcare leaders at all levels. I regularly meet and work with leaders who need more support to create an engaging work environment and help employees cope with rampant and rapid change. Another recent study, by ACCOR Services, found that 90 percent of the leaders surveyed said engagement directly impacts their business' success, yet 75 percent of leaders have no engagement strategy.[ii] And that is precisely why I wrote this book!

6 Shortcuts to Employee Engagement **offers healthcare leaders a fresh, proactive approach to employee engagement that is realistic, manageable and proven.** A shortcut is a quicker, more efficient way to get somewhere or to get something done. Don't worry; the shortcuts I share aren't shortcuts that diminish quality or service. In fact, just the opposite is true. These shortcuts lead to improved patient care and satisfaction (as well as a positive increase in metrics across the board) because they treat the *cause* of employee disengagement not just the *symptoms*. They aren't Band-Aids. They provide the long-term cure for employee disengagement. And isn't that what you're really looking for – positive, sustainable, long-term change?

This book is different than other books about employee engagement in that there's no need to "start from scratch." Many experts suggest that if you want to improve employee engagement, you need to follow their specific program or prescribed process. But in the ever-changing world of healthcare, these "flavor of the month" initiatives tend to fall by the wayside when priorities shift or things get busy. I'm suggesting another shortcut – instead of doing something *additional* that you don't have time for anyway, you can create a more engaging environment *in conjunction* with what you're already doing.

> **You will get better results faster and with less effort when you layer employee engagement concepts onto the framework of your existing systems and processes.**

To help you accomplish that, I've loaded the book with easy-to-use resources for quickly incorporating engagement concepts into your daily activities:

✦ **Team exercises** help you share specific ideas with your team so they can put them into practice with ease.

 ✦ A **Bonus Tools section** includes 12 turnkey tools, tips, scripts, exercises and assessments to streamline application.

✦ **Access to four free videos** allows you to "plug and play" at team meetings so that you save time and energy.

Please read the whole book before you start implementing the shortcuts. The book is brief by design so that you can easily read all of it. (It should take you less than two hours to finish.) Once you've read the whole book, commit to doing the team exercise in the "It Takes 3" chapter titled, "*Whose Job Is It to Make You Happy at Work?*" It will have the biggest impact on engagement. It's first for a reason – it's the foundation. Then, you'll want to triage the challenges your team is facing and decide which shortcuts to explore. Look for ideas that provide the highest impact and return. Better yet, get the team involved in the decision-making when it makes sense.

I do want to caution you about one thing. You may be very excited about the ideas we are discussing and think it's a good idea to do a "deep dive" into employee engagement by implementing many of the ideas all at once. *Please don't!* Team members will be leery and think this is another "flavor of the month" endeavor. Resist the temptation to jump in and start making wholesale changes right away. A little introspection goes a long way toward pacing yourself and prioritizing the shortcuts. Oftentimes, slow is better than fast. Let team members process the information, implement change and create a new, positive habit before moving on to the next idea. It will take time. That's okay. We're going for the kind of change that is sustainable over time.

Focusing on employee engagement puts you in a position to lead the transformation of healthcare and enjoy your job while you're doing it. Sound too good to be true? I promise it isn't. These six shortcuts, implemented over time, will put you at an advantage for achieving every outcome you seek.

It Takes 3™

Since "employee engagement" is a big buzzword these days and because this is a book about shortcuts, I'm going to save time and assume that you already know about the benefits of having engaged employees on your team. In addition to the specific benefits for healthcare organizations that we've already talked about, there are volumes of research to support the idea that engaged employees are more productive and creative and generate better results. Just search "benefits of employee engagement" on the Internet if you want more information.

While almost everyone agrees that employee engagement is beneficial, there is not as much clarity about what "employee engagement" means. According to Modern Survey's March 2013 National Employee Engagement Study, only 49 percent of employees clearly understand the concept of employee engagement. Even more surprising, just 63 percent of leaders with direct reports said they understood what engagement is.[iii] That mirrors what I see in my work with clients.

Some people think engagement means simply being happy at work. That's a good start, but it is more than that. Aon Hewitt, a global consulting firm that has done a tremendous amount of research about engagement, describes it this way: "Engagement is the emotional and intellectual commitment of an individual to build and sustain strong business performance."[iv] I actually like that definition, but I think we need a simpler, easier-to-understand description of engagement.

In my first book, *SHIFT to Professional Paradise: 5 Steps to Less Stress, More Energy & Remarkable Results at Work*, I describe employee engagement as being **satisfied, energized and productive at work.** I find that the notion of being satisfied, energized and productive is almost universally accepted and something that just about everyone can agree on. Let's take a closer look at those three descriptors:

✦ **Satisfied** is about being psychologically connected with our work. The brain is involved – we get some kind of positive emotional payoff from what we do day in and day out.

✦ **Energized** means being willing to put forth effort over time. We behave in ways that demonstrate a high energy level, such as creative thinking, going above and beyond when necessary, giving discretionary effort and working at an efficient pace.

✦ **Productive** means our efforts contribute to the overall vision and bottom line of the organization. We operate with an ownership mindset and are focused on doing work that helps patients, internal customers and the organization.

Most people inherently want to be satisfied, energized and productive at work; they just don't call it "being engaged." They genuinely want to contribute and make a positive difference for those they serve, and as a leader, you can tap into this internal motivation. They want to make positive connections with patients or internal customers and co-workers. And they want to feel appreciated on a regular basis through thought, word and deed.

Executives and leaders talk about "employee engagement"…team members don't. Most people don't wake up in the morning and say, "I want to be engaged at work today." The concept of employee engagement often gets a bad rap on the frontlines because employees see engagement as being a "win" for the organization or for patients, but not for themselves. Some employees perceive that engagement is important to the organization, and leaders primarily because it's a way to get more work and productivity out of them. That needs to change! As leaders, we need to help employees understand that when they are satisfied, energized and productive at work, everyone wins, including them.

I find that employees relate more to the idea of being satisfied, energized and productive – or what I call "Professional Paradise™" – than engagement. The concept of Professional Paradise answers the "what's in it for me" question that employees have about engagement. In Professional Paradise, the employee benefits just as much as the organization and patients. Unfortunately, far too few employees today actually enjoy Professional Paradise. Modern Survey's March 2013 National Employee Engagement Study found that only 12 percent of healthcare workers are fully engaged.[v] That means **only 1 in 10 of your employees is consistently satisfied, energized and productive.** OUCH!

The same survey found that 28 percent of healthcare workers (or 1 in every 4 of your employees) are actively disengaged.[vi] Don't believe for a minute that you don't have disengaged employees on your team and that they aren't costing you money. Every leader does. Think of employees on your team who are perpetual complainers – they never seem to be happy regardless of what happens around them. They are minimally productive, disconnected, self-focused and often angry or disruptive. These folks are members of what I call the Chain Gang, and they have sentenced themselves to Professional Prison. In other words, they choose to be disengaged.

As you've probably guessed, most people fall somewhere in the middle, between Professional Prison and Professional Paradise. The Modern Survey mentioned above found that 60 percent of healthcare workers are only moderately engaged or under engaged.[vii] These people are on Professional Parole – they have the potential to change their behaviors and make a positive difference on your team, with some direction and accountability. They are definitely worth spending your time and energy on, so show them some love!

You may think that the idea of Professional Paradise is unrealistic or even hokey, but it resonates with employees. And if we are going to ask them to be accountable for their own engagement, we need to use languaging that works for them. Asking employees to commit to "being engaged" is vague and lackluster and likely won't produce consistent results. On the other hand, asking employees to commit to being satisfied, energized and productive at work every day is both motivating and empowering. The idea of Professional Paradise gives people a goal, something to shoot for.

In a nutshell, employee engagement, being satisfied, energized and productive, and Professional Paradise are three ways to refer to the same thing. They are all one in the same:

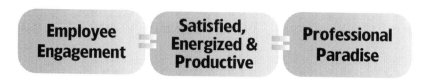

Now that we have a clearer understanding of what it is, let's talk about how we can optimize employee engagement in your organization and on your team.

The Missing Piece in the Engagement Puzzle

Over the last decade, billions of dollars and millions of hours have been invested by organizations across the country to foster greater employee engagement, yet employee *disengagement* is still at or near an all-time high. Why? Because we've been missing a key piece of the engagement puzzle: the employees!

The solution to the employee engagement problem is threefold. It Takes 3 to create sustainable engagement:

1. **An organization** that deliberately and consistently supports employee engagement at the strategic level;

2. **Leaders** who regularly drive engagement at the tactical level;

3. **Individuals** who are accountable for engagement at a personal level.

> **What's missing in most discussions about engagement is the individual employee's personal responsibility for his or her own engagement.**

For years, experts and organizations have focused on the first two areas and their role in engagement. Until recently, there was very little focus on employees taking responsibility for their own engagement. Consider the typical employee engagement survey questions. Are they focused equally on the employee's role in creating engagement for themselves? Usually not. (But they should be.)

Unfortunately, organizations and their leaders have been misguided to believe that it's their job – and theirs only – to engage employees.

That's not the case. As a leader, you are indeed a powerful influencer of engagement. Your organization has to be committed to creating a culture of engagement as well. Yet no matter how supportive the organization might be and how engaging a leader you are, you will never be able to engage an employee who doesn't want to be engaged. **It is only when team members choose to be engaged and accept responsibility for their own engagement that we can achieve sustainable results.** This is powerful, and it's time we acknowledged that truth.

In the It Takes 3™ model, engagement is represented by the point in the center where the organization, leader and employee circles all overlap. The organization and leaders are purposefully shown on the bottom because these two are foundational – they support engagement. All three circles are the same size to show that

It Takes 3™

all three elements are equally responsible. In addition, there's give-and-take between each component (Organization to Leaders; Leaders to Individuals; and, Organization to Individuals).

Let's look at these three elements in more detail:

1. **An optimized organization that deliberately and consistently supports engagement at the strategic level.** You may be thinking this is very obvious. I agree. Yet when I talk with healthcare leaders across the country and ask them about their strategic initiatives regarding engagement, I get "umms" and "ahhs." These leaders are not able to clearly

articulate their organization's strategies that focus on engagement, and if they can't articulate them, they probably aren't being consistently implemented or measured. Can your leadership group identify your organization's strategic engagement initiatives?

Healthcare businesses that are successful in creating a culture of engagement have a strong and compelling mission/vision that drives behavior. Not long ago, I was with a group of nursing leaders who weren't able to convey their organization's mission without referring to their badge. The mission was about six sentences long – no wonder they couldn't articulate it. It wasn't compelling – in fact, it was confusing. What is your mission? Does it compel employees to be engaged?

From a strategic perspective, other important elements of sustainable engagement include fair compensation and benefits and working in a safe environment (physically and psychologically). In addition, open and honest communication from executive and frontline leaders is the foundation for employees to feel a positive connection to work. The final element of an optimized organization is the opportunity for growth and development. These are all must-haves at the organizational level for sustainable employee engagement.

2. **Leaders who regularly drive engagement at the tactical level.** When it comes to engagement, a leader's primary job is to "grease the wheels" for team member engagement and help them develop accountability for their own engagement. But distractions abound that pull leaders away from a focus on engagement, and this is a problem that is evidenced over time through unwanted turnover, employee complaints and low morale. **Leaders who embrace employee engagement as**

a key priority will meet their goals faster and more productively.

Engaging leaders regularly measure and monitor employee engagement; they don't wait for a biannual survey to determine levels of engagement. In addition, they work to create positive connections with each member of their team through one-on-one meetings, daily rounding with staff, huddles and interactive team meetings. They also purposefully focus on the positive actions and outcomes of staff and celebrate their success.

Effective leaders are not afraid to call a challenge a challenge and work to minimize the challenges that are within their control. I often see leaders try to put a positive spin on big changes, but employees just don't buy in. Transformational leaders understand the ramifications of these changes and are open and honest about the work it will take to move forward.

3. **Individuals who are accountable for engagement at a personal level.** It's not enough to focus only on the organization's and leaders' roles in creating engagement. Each individual must own engagement at a personal level. Without question, external factors (such as the culture of the organization, pay and benefits, the team leader's support, etc.) play a key role in engagement. However, ultimately, engagement is an internal issue – each of us decides to be engaged or disengaged, energized or apathetic. It's not something that someone does to us. It's a choice each of us makes every day. All three elements are necessary.

We've been tiptoeing around the individual accountability piece of engagement for quite some time; employees already conceptually "get it."

Modern Survey, in the "State of Engagement" report for U.S. employees shared that "17 percent of employees hold themselves primarily accountable for being engaged on the job."[viii] In addition, 39 percent of respondents said that a combination of direct managers, senior leaders and employees are equally responsible. That's over half of employees. When I ask at team meetings, the majority usually responds that they as individuals are responsible.

What this tells me is that some employees are open to and accepting of the idea that being engaged is their responsibility and that sometimes it's probably just easier to blame leadership or to want someone else to take responsibility. The bottom line is that you have to have the discussion or you won't know. You need to ask and listen to see what *your* team thinks because that's the team that matters to you. As leaders, we have an opportunity to shift beliefs and mindsets when we facilitate a discussion that creates the awareness that It Takes 3 for engagement. In the end, everyone benefits when individuals "own" their own engagement.

Recently, when talking with a very engaging nurse leader about her daily rounding with team members, I asked her to share the questions she asks each employee. She told me she asks about how the person's day is going, what resources he or she needs and what obstacles she can help remove. I suggested that she add this question to her rounding: "What are you doing today to feel positively connected to your job?" She loved the idea, and I bet her employees did, too.

We have to stop promoting the idea that it's someone else's job to make folks happy at work. Instead, let's promote shared responsibility for engagement and encourage team members to be accountable for their own engagement. I call this being the Chief Paradise Officer (CPO) of your job. People universally love this idea. After all, who doesn't want to work in Professional Paradise and be a Chief Paradise Officer?

When team members decide to become the CPO of their job, they make conscious choices to be more engaged. They come to work with the intention of being satisfied, energized and productive. And, they support this intention with purposeful actions that drive positive outcomes, even on challenging days. I know you can picture your CPOs as I describe them. They are your high performers or superstars; they are in your succession plans. They are very valuable to your department and organization, and you want them to stay.

When it comes to engagement, our goal as leaders is to get every team member to commit to being the CPO of their job. Think about it…we have the CEO, CFO, CNO, CIO, CHRO and others, each focused on a specific area of the business. **Doesn't it make sense to have CPOs, too – people who are focused on engagement, the most significant driver of organizational results?** Imagine adding the Chief Paradise Officer title to everyone's business card or name badge. As a leader, just imagine leading a team of Chief Paradise Officers – now that would be a good day at work!

Shared Responsibility

Below is a framework I use to implement the It Takes 3 model in client organizations. It outlines the key elements that organizations need to implement at the strategic level, leaders need to carry out at the tactical level, and individuals need to execute at the personal level to create a culture of engagement. It also highlights the fact that everyone in the organization – the executive team and board, you and your leadership peers, and every team member – is all part of the long-term engagement solution.

Organization (Strategic)	Leaders (Tactical)	Individuals (Personal)
1. Commit to a strategic focus on engagement	1. Embrace Employee Engagement	1. Discover Professional Paradise
2. Live the mission, vision & values	2. Create Connections	2. Manage Your Mindset
3. Ensure a safe environment	3. Shrink Team POWs	3. Shrink Your POWs
4. Provide fair compensation & benefits	4. Grow Team WOWs	4. Grow Your WOWs
5. Communicate openly & honestly	5. *SHIFT* Team POWS to WOWs	5. *SHIFT* Your POWS to WOWs
6. Provide opportunities for growth & development	6. Measure & Monitor	6. Own It!

The middle column of this chart is the focus of this book. In fact, the six elements shown for leaders are the six shortcuts that we will discuss in detail in the following chapters. The rest of this book is all about helping you create an engaging environment for your team, communicating to team members that they have a shared responsibility for engagement, and then supporting them as they own their part of engagement. These are the areas that are within your control as a leader. Remember that song, "I've Got the Power" from the early '90s? That's what I want you to remember as you read. Keep thinking about what you have the power to impact and put your energy there.

It is crucial, however, for you to understand that as a leader, you do double duty when it comes to engagement. You are responsible not only for the leadership part of engagement but also for the individual part (the second and third columns in the chart or the Leader and Individual spheres in the model). As a leader, it is your job to create an engaging environment and help team members connect to what gets them engaged.

Equally important, as an individual contributor, *you* must be engaged in your work and role model being satisfied, energized and productive. **Every person in the organization – from the frontlines to the C-suite – must become the Chief Paradise Officer of his or her job and "own" personal engagement.** (For more on how to be personally accountable for engagement and create your own Professional Paradise, check out *SHIFT to Professional Paradise: 5 Steps to Less Stress, More Energy & Remarkable Results at Work*.)

If you are a senior-level leader, you have the added responsibility (and privilege) of doing triple duty. You are responsible for all three columns or all three spheres in the model. In addition to being personally engaged and leading an engaged team of direct reports, you also impact the organization's strategic approach to engagement. Hopefully, this is part of what gets you satisfied, energized and productive every day.

So how do shared responsibility and the It Takes 3 concept play out in an organization? Town hall meetings are just one small example. Imagine this: At your organization's next town hall meeting, the CEO kicks off the session by talking about strategies being offered at the organizational level, namely expanded tuition reimbursement and executive leadership rounding. Then, directors of three different departments discuss how they are implementing one-on-one meetings for all staff and including engagement in daily huddles and lean daily management rituals. Finally, the employees divide into small groups and share best practices of how they stay satisfied, energized and productive despite the challenges around them. The CEO asks for folks to report out, and small prizes are awarded. A collective WOW is given for each person who shares. Now that's what I call a town hall meeting with pizzazz…and an organization on its way to sustained success!

Team Exercise
Whose Job Is It to Make You Happy at Work?

The first team exercise is critical for getting buy-in around who is responsible for employee engagement. Asking for input from team members allows them to focus on their own beliefs and mindsets to form their own conclusions about engagement. This method works far better than telling employees what you want them to think and expecting them to agree. At the end of this exercise, team members will be able to:

✦ Define employee engagement.
✦ Prioritize who is responsible for their engagement.
✦ Agree on key elements of creating a culture of engagement.

To save you time and make this easy, I've created shortcuts for facilitating this exercise:

1. Plug & Play – At your next team meeting, simply play a video I've already created and let me facilitate for you.
2. Plan & Present – Use the Leader's Guide in the BONUS TOOLS section to adapt the exercise to your needs and facilitate the meeting yourself.

You can access the video and Bonus Tools at
www.**6ShortcutsToEngagement**.com

Shortcut #1:
Embrace Employee Engagement

Most leaders don't think about engagement on a daily basis. Do you?

Some leaders are forced to think about it in response to external factors such as turnover, low morale or poor engagement survey results. Others simply tolerate it or ignore it altogether. Why? Because engagement feels "soft" and people don't always clearly understand the real value behind an engaged workforce. Or it's something that no one is paying attention to or measuring on a regular basis. Unfortunately, in many organizations, it's just not something that is strategically and proactively embraced. That's got to change. That's why the first shortcut is to embrace employee engagement.

Dictionary.com defines embrace as "to take or receive gladly or eagerly; accept willingly." I realize that "embrace" is a strong word with a very positive intent behind it, one that isn't used at work very often. That's exactly why I use it here. If you want to reap the benefits of employee engagement, you need to change your mindset about engagement and accept it as foundational to everything else you do. There's a strong and direct connection between levels of engagement and financial health, patient satisfaction, safety, quality, efficiency, and so much more. Because of this, you literally need to embrace the value and importance of engagement.

Embracing engagement as an organization, as a team and as individuals is the fastest way to achieve better patient care and better business results.

So what does it mean to "embrace" engagement? It means we need to change the way we think about engagement, because that is the underpinning of all the other shortcuts. This shortcut involves taking proactive steps to change the collective mindset by understanding how beliefs impact engagement, creating a shared vocabulary and learning what specifically gets each team member satisfied, energized and productive.

Understand How Beliefs Impact Engagement

Our beliefs are a key influencer of engagement. Beliefs determine our state of mind, and our state of mind directs our actions, which in turn drive outcomes. When it comes to employee engagement,

being aware of how our beliefs help or hinder our actions and outcomes is huge.

Many people believe that being engaged at work is dependent on the organization, the job, the boss, the salary or the working environment. All of these are definitely contributing factors, but they are not the determining factor. That is why you will find plenty of disengaged people who work in fantastic jobs with great pay at exceptional companies. It's also why there are people who believe they work in Professional Paradise in jobs and conditions that most of us would find objectionable. Being satisfied, energized and productive is an internal issue based on our beliefs.

Each person on your team comes to work with beliefs that act as a lens through which they see, experience and interpret every event, situation, interaction and circumstance. If you pay attention, you will start to understand what team members believe about engagement (and other subjects, as well) by their actions. Someone who does a lot of finger pointing and blaming is showing a belief that says, "I'm not responsible for outcomes. I'm a victim." Someone who is a self-starter and solves problems independently demonstrates a belief of self-sufficiency and independence.

This first shortcut is all about examining you and your team's beliefs and mindset about engagement and changing them if you're not getting the results you want. You actually took the first steps to doing that with the first team exercise designed to expand people's thinking about who is responsible for engagement (i.e., It Takes 3).

When everyone connects with the belief that we are each responsible for our own engagement, a different mindset is developed, which drives different actions and outcomes. In other words, the disengaged are much more likely to reassess their engagement and potentially reconnect to a sense of ownership. Those who are in Professional Prison or on Professional Parole will see the possibility of Professional Paradise and understand their role in creating it or they will leave.

If you're worried that you have to become a workplace psychologist, don't be. Without spending too much time or effort, seek to understand your team's underlying beliefs and mindsets about engagement so that they can position themselves for being satisfied, energized and productive without any external prompting. Simply start paying attention and listening to what folks believe and consider how it impacts their work. Observe people's behaviors and think about the beliefs that might be driving those actions. When you notice actions that you want to see either more or less of, ask the team member questions about his or her mindset or beliefs behind the actions. It's an interesting and productive conversation to embark upon.

Create a Shared Vocabulary

In the previous chapter, we established that employee engagement, the state of being satisfied, energized and productive and Professional Paradise are synonymous.

I'm hoping that you also agree that people don't wake up every morning and say, "I want to be engaged at work today." So let's stop talking with employees about "engagement." Since the term "employee engagement" resonates well with executives and leaders but not most team members, let's create a shared vocabulary that looks at it from the employee's point of view.

To create transformation over time, it's crucial to talk about employee engagement in terms that everyone can relate to. It may seem like it doesn't matter what you call it, but it does. When you create a shared vocabulary for employee engagement, you create a vehicle for everyone to talk about it openly and comfortably.

Being satisfied, energized and productive is language that everyone – from the frontlines to the C-suite – can relate to. When conducting research for my first book, *SHIFT to Professional Paradise*, I asked more than a thousand people, "What makes you happy at work?" The largest percentage of responses related to getting things done, being productive, making a difference. It just makes sense to focus on things that your team members want to do at work every day. The biggest benefits of engagement are for team members themselves. That's the truly exciting part.

If you completed the first team exercise, employees should now understand that It Takes 3 to create sustained engagement and that they are accountable for their own engagement. Now we want to create a shared vocabulary around engagement so that everyone is on the same page. You can use "satisfied, energized and productive" or "Professional Paradise," whichever resonates more with your team. Or, if you already have common terminology that you use related to engagement, by all means use that. Just remember that the goal is to have a common vocabulary around engagement that employees can relate to.

Team Exercise
Would You Like to Work in Professional Paradise?

Use this exercise during a team meeting to create a shared vocabulary for engagement with your team. At the end of this exercise, team members will be able to:

+ Define employee engagement.
+ Share examples of times at work when they are satisfied, energized and productive.

Again, you have two options for facilitating this exercise:

1. Plug & Play – At your next team meeting, simply play a video I've already created and let me facilitate for you.
2. Plan & Present – Use the Leader's Guide in the BONUS TOOLS section to adapt the exercise to your needs and facilitate the meeting yourself.

You can access the video and Bonus Tools at
www.6ShortcutsToEngagement.com

Learn What Gets Team Members Satisfied, Energized & Productive

Another step in helping team members be accountable for their own engagement is coaching them to identify and connect with what gets them satisfied, energized and productive in a one-on-one setting. When you have a personal discussion and better understand what's motivating to an employee and his or her current level of satisfaction, you are in a better position to do something about it – and to help the employee do something as well. Note that this isn't about being a cheerleader for employees; it's about seeking to understand what the influencers of engagement are for each of the team members you lead and then helping them make the connection between those influencers and their daily work.

You started this process in the team exercise. Now it's time to go a bit deeper with each team member individually with what I call the Match Game. The Match Game is a way to proactively and purposefully match projects, committee assignments, activities and responsibilities with team members' engagement drivers.

When I worked in the Education Resource Center at LifeBridge Health, my boss and I had monthly one-on-one meetings. During one of those meetings, I shared my desire to get involved more at the system level. I let her know that I wanted to continue to grow my internal network and learn new performance-improvement strategies. With a twinkle in her eye, she graciously offered me the opportunity to serve on the Lost Wheelchair Team. This system-wide, multidisciplinary team provided me with a learning opportunity and provided my boss with a volunteer to represent our department. To most other people in my department, being assigned to the Lost Wheelchair Team would have been the same as being sentenced to a stint in Professional Prison. But for me, it was Professional

Paradise! The assignment was a perfect match with my engagement drivers. This is the Match Game in action!

When you use your knowledge of what gets team members satisfied, energized and productive to assign projects and activities, you multiply engagement throughout the team. Each team member consistently gets *more* of the kind of work that gets them satisfied, energized and productive and *less* of the work that tends to contribute to their disengagement.

To "play" the Match Game, you must first discover specifically what gets each employee satisfied, energized and productive. This can easily be done in conjunction with your existing one-on-one meetings. Or, if you're not currently holding one-on-ones with team members, simply schedule a 10- to 15-minute get-together with each of them over the next few weeks. I know you are busy, so do what's realistic based on your schedule. Just don't put this off for too long because, as I've said, this is the foundation of your engagement efforts.

Once you have all of this great information about what gets each employee satisfied, energized and productive, use it intentionally to foster more engagement. First, regularly remind team members that they can connect to these engagement influencers simply by paying attention and noticing the "paradise" parts of their day. This reinforces with employees their role in and responsibility for engagement and directly helps them identify even more of these influencers, thereby increasing their engagement.

Second, use the information to create a more engaging environment by intentionally matching employees' engagement drivers with tasks and activities that meet those criteria. This may seem like a daunting task, but it's actually quite simple and, honestly, kind of fun. The Match Game is one of the most high-impact activities for growing engagement that I am aware of. Brief instructions and tips for the Match Game can be found in the BONUS TOOLS section and can be downloaded at www.6ShortcutsToEngagement.com.

I presume that not only do you want the results that an actively engaged workforce or team can produce but you also want those results in the shortest time possible. When you take a trip, there are a number of different routes you could take – some longer, some shorter. Busy people want to reach their destination in the shortest time possible. The exercises and tips I've suggested in this shortcut provide an opportunity to bypass the long and arduous road to demystifying engagement. Embracing employee engagement is foundational since each person's beliefs and mindsets about what is engaging drive their actions and outcomes. Between the team meeting and the one-on-one follow-up, you and your team are well on your way to embracing employee engagement.

Shortcut #1:

Embrace Employee Engagement

+ Understand beliefs and mindsets.
+ Create a shared vocabulary.
+ Learn what gets people satisfied, energized and productive.

Shortcut #2:
Create Connections

Research shows that team members are more engaged when they feel a strong connection with their leader and the organization. This has been proven time after time in surveys by global HR consulting firms.

I wanted to test this hypothesis myself and dig a bit deeper, so I conducted an informal snapshot survey of my clients and newsletter readers. Not surprisingly, my findings were in line with those of prior studies: The number one thing (by a wide margin) that respondents said was very important with respect to engagement was open communication. According to other surveys I've conducted over the past three years, team members repeatedly said they want more time with their managers and would like to see their managers in their work area more often. This underscores how critical it is to create connections with your team!

Connecting with employees shouldn't be something new. I know you are doing a lot of these actions already. The shortcut here is to take what you are already doing to create connections and add an engagement component. You have to regularly and consistently talk with employees about being satisfied, energized and productive. **If you're only talking about engagement when there's a survey to conduct or results to review, team members will not feel any sense of ownership.**

In my experience, many leaders don't spend as much time connecting with team members as they should. Studies continue to show that leaders *think* they connect and communicate far more than their employees perceive they do. Almost every healthcare leader I know should spend more time connecting. Making incremental changes in your level of connection will pay high dividends for engagement.

Please stay open-minded about this shortcut. I know that many managers would rather do their "work" than spend time on the relationship side of our business. That's the challenge. Sometimes the payoff for doing non-employee-related activities, like solving a problem at your desk, is more immediate and gratifying. And non-relationship activities are often easier or more comfortable, such as answering emails versus having real conversations with staff. So many distractions exist in your day that you could easily *not* take time to connect with team members and still be "doing your job." Recognize the temptation to stay in your office to "get work done" and remind yourself how important the connection time is.

Every healthcare leader I survey, talk with or get emails from is struggling to manage his or her time. I get that. That's why this shortcut is all about shoring up your connections with your team using activities you are already doing. We'll look at your regular connection activities through the lens of employee engagement and tweak them to make small changes that will optimize engagement. This is a different way of thinking about employee engagement. Rather than a new, complex activity, this is all about adding an engagement component to things you do all of the time as part of your basic conversations.

Opportunities to create connections exist in the following venues:

✦ Regular rounding with team members;

✦ Monthly team meetings;

✦ One-on-one meetings.

Rounding

Rounding with team members is one of the best overall uses of your time when it comes to creating connections. Many of you are probably using rounding now to check on systems and processes, patient satisfaction or other technical elements of the department you manage. I'm suggesting that you add an engagement component to the rounding you are already doing. And if you aren't currently rounding, then evaluate this as one option for creating connections. It involves scheduling time on your calendar regularly (and on all shifts you supervise) to spend time with your team informally listening and observing.

Rounding allows for real-time feedback from team members on the hallmarks of engagement – satisfaction, energy and productivity. It gives you a chance to use all of your senses to determine how things are going, what needs attention and who needs recognition.

One CFO I interviewed talked about senior leader rounding as one strategy his organization put in place to improve engagement. He shared that rounding throughout the organization really changed his perspective on many things and that he's gotten to know many more members of the staff. He said, "Initially I thought it would be tough, but now I enjoy it very much." Sounds like he's found a little piece of Professional Paradise!

Some leaders are very good at this informal process. Others have asked for a tool to use. To help you add the engagement component to your rounding, I created a shortcut tool called the Traffic Light Check-In.™ This tool uses the metaphor of a traffic signal to quickly and easily gather feedback about real-time levels of engagement.

 Brief instructions and tips for the Traffic Light Check-In can be found in the BONUS TOOLS section and can be downloaded at www.6ShortcutsToEngagement.com.

Regular rounding is a perfect way for all healthcare leaders (clinical or not) to increase engagement by creating positive connections with team members on an ongoing basis.

Team Meetings

Another way to productively create connections is by conducting interactive, two-way team meetings with your direct reports. Most healthcare managers I work with have some form of regular team meeting because they understand the value of communicating information to the staff. The typical team meetings I hear about or attend involve the leader (you) standing in the front of the room, following an agenda, making announcements about important new developments or changes, and asking if there are any questions. Sound familiar?

I'm sure some of you also have team members report about areas they are focusing on, such as committees, unit councils or process improvement teams. Even with a focus on "what" to do, there is often little focus on the satisfied and energized part.

As with rounding, the key is taking what you already do – holding the team meeting – and adding the engagement component. Imagine these two very different team meetings:

◆ Meeting #1: Rick, a department manager, sends out an email asking for topic ideas for an upcoming staff meeting. No one responds, so Rick takes it upon himself to think about what to include and spends time creating the agenda. He is thoughtful and works on making this a good meeting. He sends out the agenda in advance. On the day of the meeting, he is at the front running things. He shares pertinent information from the management meeting he attended. A few people ask questions. The meeting ends on time. Everyone leaves, nothing changes, and the process repeats the next month. This is not necessarily a bad meeting, but it does nothing to capitalize on the time together to foster more engagement.

◆ Meeting #2: Rick decides to build some connection time into the meeting to get the team more involved. About a week before the scheduled meeting, as he is rounding, he uses the Traffic Light Check-In to get some feedback on current levels of engagement. While rounding, he follows up with questions about the root causes of disengagement for folks who report a "red" day and the root causes of engagement for the folks reporting a "green" day. Then Rick goes to his Match Game board and finds people who like problem solving, teaching and mentoring. He personally asks them to lead parts of the team meeting (using some of the Bonus Tools in the book) and offers his support. He also reaches out to ask someone from the education department to come and lead a team exercise so that he can participate, and they happily agree. The meeting is transformed from an information exchange to an opportunity to create connections between Rick and the team (and the team members themselves).

Including an engagement component to your current team meetings is a great way to optimize team time. To make this easier for you, there is a sample Team Meeting Agenda in the BONUS TOOLS section, or you can download it at www.6ShortcutsToEngagement.com. You don't need to start from scratch. Continue to use those elements that help you connect with team members, and pick and choose elements of my agenda that will add value.

One-on-One Meetings

Monthly one-on-one meetings with your direct reports are a high-impact way to create connections. Please don't stop reading this section because you think this is impossible or because you've tried them and "they don't work." They do. I've been asking healthcare leaders and employees their feelings on this topic for several years and I've yet to talk with anyone who doesn't agree that there is a significant return on investment for time and energy spent meeting one-on-one.

When I refer to a one-on-one meeting, I mean a meeting between you and one team member. The meeting is previously arranged, scheduled on the calendar and held in a private place with no interruptions. The meeting typically lasts between 20-30 minutes. *It is not a performance management conversation.* It's meant to be an open forum for communicating and creating connections between you and the individual.

One-on-one meetings are an efficient way to accomplish open communication, build strong relationships, encourage team member growth and development and promote teamwork. These are critical engagement activities that all leaders should focus on. If an employee knows that on a regular basis he or she will have dedicated time to talk with you in a casual environment, it contributes to a feeling of being heard and has the potential to vastly improve engagement.

Healthcare leaders tell me that the two biggest roadblocks to conducting one-on-one meetings are: 1) finding the time to meet, and 2) being unclear about what format to use. Let me take a moment to address both of these.

✦ **Timing:** I know that, realistically, it's very hard to set aside time for one-on-one meetings with team members. You spend A LOT of time in meetings and responding to email. You spend another chunk of time on problem solving, hiring, managing finances, responding to requests, talking with customers, and the list goes on. With all of that work on your daily planner, I can understand why it would seem that there's not time for focusing on creating connections to drive employee engagement.

One of the top things you can do to drive results for your team and your organization is to focus on engagement. Remember, improved engagement leads to positive results in just about all other metrics. Please don't make the mistake of replacing connection time with other work. This error in judgment will come back to haunt you. You have to make sure you are spending your time wisely and leveraging your time to foster engagement because it will pay off handsomely in positive results and few problems.

✦ **Format:** Many leaders aren't sure what they should focus on during one-on-one meetings that are not performance reviews. Great places to focus include:

◇ The areas you are addressing for your Employee Engagement Survey Action Plan.

✧ Things that are working well – Ask team members to share things that have been going well and then share your thoughts about progress on things that are going well.

✧ Things that need work – Ask for ideas and suggestions for improving the department or job, as well as possible areas of personal development.

✧ Things that require follow up – Be sure to add an accountability factor so items don't get missed moving forward.

For these meetings to be successful, you simply need to be a good listener, genuinely care about your team members, and help them meet their work goals. In addition, make this meeting about them, not you. Remember to be open and transparent so that you create, build and sustain a solid relationship with each team member. Come out from behind your desk to sit next to the employee. Be yourself, lighten up, and make it comfortable for both of you. Laughter is encouraged!

One security manager I worked with had 15 security officers reporting to him. It was challenging for him to remember what he wanted to talk about at each one-on-one meeting, so he created hanging files for each employee in his desk drawer. (You could keep a similar system on the computer. Do what works best for you.) After each one-on-one meeting, he recorded the key points and put the notes in the file to review before the next meeting. Anything that required follow-up went on his calendar. In addition, when something happened that he wanted to talk to the team member about – like the officer receiving a compliment or an interesting article that the manager wanted to share – he simply dropped it in the file folder. This list of thoughts and questions helped him prepare for the meetings and also provided other areas to discuss in case the employee didn't have a lot to talk about. This increased his confidence level and made the meetings more productive and energizing for his direct reports.

 Check the BONUS TOOLS section for a sample meeting agenda and One-on-One Meeting Grid, as well as tips on how to effectively and efficiently conduct one-on-one meetings. You'll also find specific tips for nurse managers, who often have many direct reports across multiple shifts. You can also download these tools and tips at www.6ShortcutsToEngagement.com.

When it comes to ways to positively impact employee engagement, connecting with each member of your team is critically important and a great use of your time. Consider rounding, team meetings and one-on-one meetings. Start with the areas that you think will have the highest impact for your team. Being visible, really getting to know your team members, and showing genuine interest are all ways that you create connections and improve engagement, every step of the way.

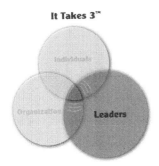

It Takes 3™

Shortcut #1: Embrace Employee Engagement

Shortcut #2: Create Connections

✦ Understand beliefs and mindsets.

✦ Create a shared vocabulary.

✦ Learn what gets people satisfied, energized and productive.

Shortcut #3:
Shrink Team POWs

If the organization is doing its part to foster engagement at the strategic level, and you are doing your part by connecting with team members and encouraging them to own their engagement, then you are well on your way to creating a culture of engagement. But even in the most engaging environments, some of the biggest drivers of disengagement are challenges, difficulties, problems and obstacles. I call these POWS.

 According to *The Random House Unabridged Dictionary*, a "pow" is "a heavy blow." Have you ever experienced a figurative heavy blow at work – an event, situation or interaction that sucker punches you, distracts you, aggravates you and just plain leaves you feeling bad? That's a POW in a nutshell. POWs get in the way of you – and your team members – being satisfied, energized and productive.

POWs are either *externally or internally* generated. Internal POWs are self-inflicted, created by team members themselves and usually stem from worry and fear. For example, reading an email and assuming something negative about the "tone" without any information to back up that assumption. Internal POWs originate in the part of our mind that worries about things before they even happen. Team members often create their own internal POWs through procrastination, negative assumptions and resistance to change. To learn how to manage your own internal POWs or to help a team member who is struggling with internal POWs, read *SHIFT to Professional Paradise: 5 Steps to Less Stress, More Energy & Remarkable Results at Work.*

Conversely, external POWs are the result of uncontrollable situations or other people's actions. They happen *to* us instead of *within* us. Examples of external POWs that affect your team might include:

+ Dealing with challenging people (patients or co-workers).
+ New regulatory requirements that affect processes or workflow.
+ New or non-functioning technology.
+ Staffing issues.
+ Financial constraints that affect staffing and resource allocation.
+ New policies and procedures.

The big problem with all POWs is that they often lead to disengagement, like ripples in a pond. Their impact extends beyond the individual experiencing them and affects patients, co-workers, internal customers, teams, and even entire organizations. Think of a recent situation in which a team member experienced a patient-related POW and took it out on another co-worker. The Chain Gang members are very good at sharing their POWs with everyone. They like the drama that is created. That's the negative ripple effect of POWs. One person's POW has the power to disengage an entire team.

Even the most highly engaged employees are prone to frustration if POWs continue over time. Broken systems and processes, irritating co-workers who "get away with" bad behavior, staffing issues and a lack of resources are common chronic POWs. Since they don't want to be seen as complainers, these employees might keep quiet and try to solve the problems themselves (if they can). If that doesn't work, they typically start looking for a new job. Take "Rosemary," for instance. Rosemary is a frustrated CPO. She is a relatively new nurse who has been working on a med-surg unit for about 18 months. She's a bit older than the typical new team member as nursing is her second career. Her manager, "Dimitri," thinks she's a "star." He is very happy with Rosemary's work ethic, clinical knowledge and internal motivation. He considers her a highly engaged, top performer…a Chief Paradise Officer.

While doing consulting work with this team, I interviewed Rosemary about her thoughts and perceptions about her job, the team and Dimitri. She was very candid about her frustrations and dislikes – including some specific complaints about Dimitri's inability to help solve recurring problems. She confidentially shared with me that she was looking for a new job even though she didn't really want to. When asked if she had shared her concerns with Dimitri, she said, "I'm still the new kid on the block. I don't want to stir up trouble."

This is a perfect example of a manager who needs to identify and shrink team POWs before the top performers leave. On a side note, the low performers on the team were equally unhappy and unproductive and were NOT looking for jobs – that's a triple POW!

As a leader, you are in a good position to help team members identify and shrink POWs. This shortcut focuses on how you can help minimize challenges that prevent your team from being satisfied, energized and productive. I'll explain how you and your team can talk about challenges in a positive and productive manner and offer specific strategies to manage the problems that inevitably arise. Let's look at the four different types of POWs and how you and the team can shrink each one.

Predictable POWs

A predictable POW is a problem or challenge that the team can anticipate – it has a trigger or direct cause. When "A" happens, then "B" is most likely to follow as a POW. The introduction of new technology (think EMR – Electronic Medical Record) is often a Predictable POW. Other predictable POWs include scheduling time off for holidays or summer vacation, new employees needing orientation, annual competency testing, technology updates, physical plant changes and CPR renewal, to name just a few.

The one good thing about a predictable POW is that you can anticipate it and, with a little forethought, you and the team can work to minimize its impact or eliminate it altogether. The shortcut is to get the team involved *before* the POW occurs to determine what is within everyone's control:

1. Identify potential triggers – situations or events that could cause a POW.
2. What are the likely negative effects of the trigger?
3. Can you minimize or eliminate the trigger? If so, how?
4. If not, brainstorm ways to manage the negative effects.

Flu season is a trigger for many winter POWs. Whether you are in direct patient care or support those who are, you likely feel the effects of the flu season when volume increases and procedures don't change. When the census is higher, there are more call-outs and work is busier. Other than encouraging the local community to get the flu shot, there's not much you can do to minimize the trigger. One engaging distribution manager put flu season on the agenda at his November team meeting. He worked with staff members to list all of the POWs that occurred the previous year as a result of flu season. As a team, they looked at what they could do differently this year. The team appreciated that he was aware of the upcoming challenges and together they came up with a "Face the Flu" plan to shrink the Predictable POWs.

Think about one or two Predictable POWs that your team members experience and jot down the triggers and ideas on how to shrink them.

Predictable POW	Trigger	Ideas to Shrink This POW or Its Impact

Perpetual POWs

Perpetual POWs repeat over and over regardless of your best efforts. Rush-hour traffic is a perfect example of a perpetual POW that you might experience personally. A Perpetual POW for every healthcare team is change — it's rapid, ongoing and often complex. Get used to it. Just like rush-hour traffic, it's here to stay. The volume of change might ebb and flow, the pace of change might speed up or slow down, but in the end, we will still be experiencing vast amounts of change. Other examples include managing last-minute staff call-outs and handling conflict between cliques on the team.

The shortcut to shrink a Perpetual POW can literally be a shortcut. One of the best ways to minimize this type of POW is to create a "work-around" or alternate plan. One way to avoid the POW of traffic is to find another route. One way to shrink the POW of constant change is to conduct training, share information and keep people updated. Another way is to benchmark how others have made improvements during various change efforts and then adopt those ideas.

Think about one or two Perpetual POWs that team members experience and jot down ideas on how to shrink them.

Perpetual POW	Ideas to Work Around or Shrink This POW

Preventable POWs

This type of POW is an internal or external situation or event that can be fixed or avoided. Procrastination is a prime example of a preventable internal POW. Putting something off until the last minute — and all the stress associated with doing that — is avoidable. External preventable POWs include lack of communication within the department due to team members not reading or responding to their email, gossiping, three-way conversations that avoid the real issue and lead to passive-aggressive behavior, bullying and so on.

Another common preventable team POW is inter-departmental conflict. When I worked as a nurse on a Post Partum unit, we used to get frustrated with the Labor & Delivery nurses when they would call in a report for a new patient at shift change or send us a couple of admissions at once. We were only seeing things through our eyes and never stopped to think about what might be going on in their department. The real POW wasn't the patient transfer; it was our misguided idea that they were "being mean" or doing it on purpose. With open communication, we could have gotten past the hurt feelings and misguided blame. As a leader, you can encourage inter-departmental communication and team building and shrink these kinds of POWs once and for all.

The shortcut to shrink Preventable POWs is similar to Predictable POWS. The process doesn't have to be long and protracted. Think shortcut:

1. Recognize the issue as a POW.

2. Determine the root causes.

3. Brainstorm ways to fix the underlying problem...and then fix it!

On a Neuro unit I worked with, the team was starting a lean process-improvement project regarding missing medications. They just couldn't understand why the pharmacy wasn't bringing the meds to the unit in a timely manner. The missing medications were a big POW that seemed preventable. During their data collection, they discovered that there were several broken processes that were affecting the delivery of medications. It was not the pharmacy's fault but a series of mishaps. By finding the root cause, they were able to work with the pharmacy to tackle this Preventable POW and shrink it once and for all. Because Preventable POWs are often also Perpetual POWs (like the missing medication), when you fix the root cause, you minimize or eliminate not just one POW but many.

Think about one or two Preventable POWs that team members experience and jot down ideas on how to shrink them.

Preventable POW	Root Cause	Ideas to Shrink This POW or Its Impact

Team Exercise
Tackle Team POWs

Now that you've thought about some of the POWs your team experiences, it's time to get their input as well with this easy exercise. Consider it an investment in the individual accountability of your team, and you will see vast returns in productivity, service, quality, etc., over time. You are planting the seeds for team members to be the Chief Paradise Officer of their job when you complete this exercise about everyone's role in shrinking POWs. At the end of this exercise, team members will be able to:

✦ List common POWs they experience and categorize them.
✦ Take action to shrink the POWs.

To save you time and make this easy, there are two options for facilitating this exercise:

1. Plug & Play – At your next team meeting, simply play a video I've already created and let me facilitate for you.
2. Plan & Present – Use the Leader's Guide below to adapt the exercise to your needs and facilitate the meeting yourself.

You can access the video and Bonus Tools at
www.**6ShortcutsToEngagement**.com

POWs You Introduce

There is one final type of POW we have to talk about. Unfortunately, as a leader, you are sometimes the one introducing the POWs. Consider this the list of things NOT to do in your daily interactions with the team:

✦ Micromanagement;

✦ Disorganization;

✦ Holding back information;

✦ Not being present in the work area;

✦ Letting people "get away with things;"

✦ Your own disengagement;

✦ Not personally greeting team members;

✦ Not listening to ideas from team members.

We'll stop here before you get too depressed. The point is to be aware of POWs that you are creating. They may be unintentional, and it's important for you to recognize how these POWs could be negatively impacting team members' engagement. The goal is to stop doing them or shrink them before they become too big.

One of the most disengaging POWs that leaders bring to the team is not holding all team members accountable. Employees want fairness and consistency, and a perceived lack of accountability for certain team members is a big POW. Let's say a Chain Gang member consistently doesn't meet expectations in terms of job performance. You can shrink the POW by holding this person accountable for his or her actions. Of course, you would never share one-on-one conversations related to job performance with other team members, but the team will see the behavior change and know that something is being done.

Another key strategy is to acknowledge the big POWs and give your team time to process them. Oftentimes, as a leader, you've been privy to or involved in making a decision about an upcoming change. You've had weeks or months to process the change and you are ready to go. Then you introduce it to the team and expect them to jump onboard right away. That's a double POW!

Leaders often mistakenly think that they shouldn't focus on problems and challenges because it will lead to more disengagement. In fact, the opposite is true. You enhance engagement when you acknowledge and validate something as a POW. Everyone on your team knows it's a problem, and if you act like it isn't, your team thinks you're clueless. Or they think you "sugar-coat" POWs when you can't do anything about them. You can actually improve engagement in spite of POWs by being authentic and calling a POW a POW. Your genuine concern and empathy goes a long way toward softening the blow of the POW. This is not the time to put your head in the sand. Jump in and help your team effectively shrink their POWs and share stress management tools to minimize the impact when they can't.

POWs have a negative impact on your team's ability to be satisfied, energized and productive. When the POWs are internal, you can provide support and encouragement for personal change. When they are external, you are in a great position to have a positive impact in shrinking or eliminating them.

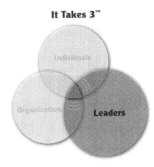

It Takes 3™

Shortcut #1: Embrace Employee Engagement

Shortcut #2: Create Connections

Shortcut #3: Shrink Team POWs

✦ Problems, challenges and obstacles – or POWs – can lead to disengagement in even the most engaging environments.

✦ Work with your team to identify the biggest POWs that affect them.

✦ Strategize ways to minimize the team POWs.

✦ Take action to shrink or eliminate them completely.

Shortcut #4:
Grow Team WOWs

We discovered in the last chapter how shrinking POWs leads to higher employee engagement. But what about the other end of the spectrum? What about the successes, wins, victories and other great things that happen to us at work? I call these WOWs. This shortcut is all about focusing on and celebrating the positive things going on, because **when you and the team grow WOWs, you grow engagement.**

A "wow" is a joyous exclamation. *Merriam-Webster Dictionary* also defines "wow" as "a sensational hit or a striking success." A "wow" as I define it is any event, situation, interaction or experience that creates a positive outcome, result or emotion. WOWs get you jazzed. They create joy, delight and pleasure. When you have a WOW, you feel like you're in the zone, at the top of your game, performing at your peak. You are energized, your stress level is low, and you have a skip in your step.

Like POWs, WOWs come in two varieties – internal and external. External WOWs happen as a result of other people or outside circumstances and situations. Examples of external WOWs include a co-worker pitching in to help, an executive acknowledging our efforts or a patient or internal customer complimenting us. Receiving appreciation is a common external WOW that people seek out in their day-to-day work. On the other hand, internal WOWs come from within. Their source is our viewpoint or our response to certain things. Feeling fulfilled when serving someone else, solving a problem, or coming up with a great idea are examples of internal WOWs.

Chief Paradise Officers are good at recognizing external WOWs and growing internal ones. Since each of us has the power to create Professional Paradise – connecting ourselves to what gets us satisfied, energized and productive – growing WOWs is a key skill that each team member needs to develop. In this shortcut, the focus is on your leadership role in growing external WOWs for others and helping your direct reports grow their own internal WOWs. The ideas can be easily tailored for your style, the team's personality and the overall culture of your organization so that everyone enjoys work more and is more productive. You may think the suggestions feel "basic." Successful leaders know that basics form the foundation for a positive culture.

Here are 12 specific suggestions to grow team WOWs. Pick a few that will have the biggest impact with your direct reports and make them part of your routine.

1. Pitch in to help.

Whether this means taking vital signs, manning the help desk call center or something specific to your work area, the people who report to you want to know that you understand their job and are willing to help when needed. This not only grows WOWs, it also shrinks POWs and contributes positively to meeting your department's goals.

2. Be honest about challenges and problems.

Your team doesn't want a parent at work; they want a partner. They don't need you to "protect" them from bad news. In fact, the opposite is true. Keeping team members abreast of challenges that lie ahead and involving them as partners in problem solving is a big WOW. Parent and partner share six of the same letters. The extra "R" in partner must stand for the respect you show your team by including them in what's happening.

3. Show genuine interest in team members' lives and share your outside pursuits with them.

Learning more about what gets folks satisfied, energized and productive, both at work and at home, helps to form positive relationships. Sharing your own interests with others shows the human side of your leadership role. I once worked with a team that said their manager was "so private" and "never shared anything about himself." This leader was a self-identified introvert who thought it was best to keep work and home separate. The staff, however, thought he was standoffish. Opening up and getting to know others builds trust and grows WOWs.

4. Help people do what they love.

Once you are clear about what gets employees satisfied, energized and productive, the Match Game (mentioned in Shortcut #1) is a perfect way to grow WOWs. Instead of guessing at what people would enjoy, ask them or use assessment tools to find out. Years of research from the Gallup Organization, shared in several books about utilizing strengths at work, reinforces the idea that leaders need to help team members identify and optimize what they enjoy and what they do best (acknowledging that these might be different things).

5. Let people see the passion you have for your work.

Growing your own WOWs and sharing them with your team makes a big difference for those around you. Do you remember why you took your job in the first place? Think back to your first few months on the job when you were satisfied, energized and productive. Think about how things have changed for the better (or worse) since then and consciously look at how you can capitalize on the current WOWs. If you need more help with this, re-read your copy of *SHIFT to Professional Paradise*.

6. Look for incremental progress.

Feeling satisfied for making progress on a project is a major internal WOW. Teresa Amabile and Steven Kramer, authors of *The Progress Principle*, conducted research that analyzed 12,000 daily surveys filled out by participants regarding their workday. Here's what they found: "When we compared our research participants' best and worst days…we found that the most common event triggering a 'best day' was any progress in the work by the individual or the team. The most common event triggering a 'worst day' was a setback."[ix] This is tangible evidence that confirms the power of the progress WOW (and the power of the setback POW). Help your team identify and celebrate incremental progress on projects, processes and goals.

7. Admit your mistakes and own up to what will change moving forward.

I was awed in a team meeting at a client organization when a physical therapy manager stood in front of her entire team and apologized for mistakes she had made in the past. The team had given her some tough feedback in a survey and she owned her part of the issues they brought up. She asked for a clean slate and offered one for each team member as well. The unit is re-energized and trust is being rebuilt. Accepting responsibility for our mistakes – and encouraging others to do the same – is a WOW.

And the Survey Says...

Several times over the years, I have asked people in informal surveys to respond to this question: *"Name one or two things your manager has done in the last month that help you to be more satisfied, energized and productive at work."* Here are some of the verbatim responses. Notice that they aren't complex, expensive or hard to implement. This is "low-hanging fruit" – in other words, easy ways to grow WOWs for your team.

✦ *Pushed back against customers, in support of decisions I made. The feeling of empowerment and that your leadership will support you goes a long way.*

✦ *Gives me the freedom to do my job and find the solutions that best fit our clients.*

✦ *Communicated priorities and supported my work-life balance as needed.*

✦ *Included me early in the decision and planning process for projects. Provided opportunities for me to develop my interests and be involved in activities not strictly related to my core work.*

✦ *Provided knowledgeable feedback and insights.*

✦ *Being willing to listen to how we do things (he's new to the organization) and asking, "What value does this add to the organization?" A fresh perspective is helping to challenge the "way we've always done it."*

✦ *Took the time to get back up to speed on payroll processing so I can take the day off to go to a seminar that I really want to attend – otherwise I wouldn't be able to go.*

✦ *She asked me to take on a fun task that is not really in my specific department. She also asked my opinion on a subject outside of my expertise area – it made me feel valued.*

8. Appreciate people more than you think you need to.
We hear all of the time about the value of appreciation, yet employees regularly talk about a lack of it. But the need for appreciation is not isolated to employees. My leadership audiences also long for more recognition. It seems that most of us yearn for external recognition to validate our internal WOWs or grow our external ones. Taking the time to appreciate each and every staff member on a regular basis shows that you value the specific contributions each makes. Whether it's a thank-you note, a candy bar or a literal pat on the back, the gesture speaks loudly as a foundational WOW.

9. Give team members autonomy to get the job done.
Micromanagement is a big POW. Autonomy is a big WOW. Stop interfering with work processes and let employees do their best work their way (of course, if safety is involved, you'll need to jump in). I had a boss once who nitpicked the slides I'd created for a presentation. He didn't like the color I'd chosen and wanted a bar chart instead of a pie chart. Come on – really? That happened 30 years ago and I still remember it. Celebrate the WOWs that are your direct reports' creative solutions instead of dwelling on how you would have done it better.

10. Capitalize on teachable moments.
Giving folks autonomy to get the job done doesn't mean abdicating your responsibility to teach and help them grow. Do you share your talents when team members are ready and willing to learn? Remember why you were put into this leadership role in the first place. Most likely it was because you excelled at the same job that your direct reports are now doing. Use your valuable years of experience to create WOWs for your team. I loved it when my bosses helped me do a better job. Knowing

they were taking the time to teach me what they did so well was a huge WOW.

11. Invite people into your leadership world.

For employees who show leadership potential or voice an interest in learning about your job, offer to have them tag along with you. Invite them to internal or external meetings, explain the budget process, talk about performance improvement indicators, nominate them to chair a committee, or have them join you while rounding. They will see things from a different perspective and create WOWs for themselves, their customers and their co-workers.

12. Celebrate moments of gratitude.

This might sound a bit "soft" to some of you, but there's serious scientific data to support a regular practice of gratitude. Robert Emmons, a professor at the University of California-Davis and author of *THANKS!: How Practicing Gratitude Can Make You Happier* (Houghton-Mifflin), has done quite a bit of research about the benefits of gratitude. He reports on one study that showed that ".... grateful people report higher levels of positive emotions, life satisfaction, vitality, optimism and lower levels of depression and stress. The disposition toward gratitude appears to enhance pleasant feeling states more than it diminishes unpleasant emotions."[x] Notice that he doesn't say grateful people are total optimists who don't see the "real" world with all its blemishes. Share what you are grateful for and encourage others to do the same. Making gratitude a regular practice is a high-impact way to grow team WOWs every day.

Team Exercise
The WOW Challenge

In the shortcut about POWs, you spent time focusing on the challenges in your area. This team exercise focuses on the WOWs! The WOW Challenge is a contest that rewards individuals who uncover team WOWs on a regular basis. At the end of this challenge, team members will be able to:

◆ List common team WOWs that they experience.
◆ Describe ways to grow more WOWs.

To save you time and make this easy, there are two options for facilitating this exercise:

1. Plug & Play – At your next team meeting, simply play a video I've already created and let me facilitate for you.
2. Plan & Present – Use the Leader's Guide in the BONUS TOOLS section to adapt the exercise to your needs and facilitate the meeting yourself.

You can access the video and Bonus Tools at
www.**6ShortcutsToEngagement**.com

Perhaps the coolest thing about a WOW is that you can use your body to create a visual symbol. When something great happens or you experience an internal WOW, take both hands and make a "W" out of your first 3 fingers. Hold your hands up on each side of your face and slap on a big grin. Voila! You have created a living, breathing WOW sign. Be sure to say "WOW" when you do the motions. Caution – this will make you look goofy. It's okay. Let down your guard and have some fun. It is actually quite liberating because then everyone won't think you are perfect and you can stop trying to live up to those expectations. Now that's a WOW!

The road to Professional Paradise is paved with WOWs. There are hundreds of ways to grow team WOWs. These 12 are just a few. The key is to focus on what is going right. Growing team WOWs has a positive ripple effect on patients and internal customers, other leaders and you. And…everyone ends up being more satisfied, energized and productive!

Stephanie Diedericks and Vicki showing the WOW sign!

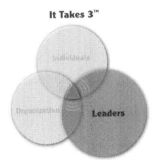

It Takes 3™

Shortcut #1: Embrace Employee Engagement

Shortcut #2: Create Connections

Shortcut #3: Shrink Team POWs

Shortcut #4: Grow Team WOWs

✦ Focusing on and celebrating successes (WOWs) grows engagement.

✦ Help employees connect internally to what gets them satisfied, energized and productive.

✦ Proactively look for ways to grow external WOWs for your team every day.

Shortcut #5:
SHIFT Team POWs to WOWs

Up to this point, we've been talking about things you can do in your leadership role to shrink team POWs and grow team WOWs. These are important skills to have because they are key aspects to creating an engaging environment. Unfortunately, there will be times when POWs hit the team despite all of your best efforts. Tough customers, changing regulations, financial concerns and staffing issues (to name just a few) are a fact of life in healthcare.

When these unavoidable POWs crop up, they can be big distractions that lead to big decreases in productivity. In addition, work teams sometimes have a "herd" mentality where Chain Gang members drag the rest of the team along with them to Professional Prison. Disengagement is contagious (fortunately, so is engagement). Your role as a leader is to help your team manage POWs in a way that moves everyone in a positive direction rather than continuing to focus on the problem.

This shortcut provides a proven process for helping team members turn challenges into positive outcomes. Systems and processes improve productivity and positive outcomes. The five-step *SHIFT* process is perfect for dealing with the human side of large and small problems at an acute or systemic level. It's logical, memorable, accessible, and it works!

SHIFT is an acronym that describes a proprietary technique that I've developed to change ineffective, detrimental thought patterns and their resulting actions to positive, beneficial thought patterns, actions and habits. It's a way of looking at situations and events differently and making the necessary adjustments to create a better outcome. In other words, **SHIFT is a series of steps anyone can use to transform any POW to a WOW** (or somewhere close). It's definitely more than just positive thinking. *SHIFT* involves discovering where disconnects are and making deliberate changes to get back on track. The outcomes of using *SHIFT* with the team are more positive connections with co-workers and customers, vastly improved performance and results, less stress and more energy. In short, the outcome is that team members can get back to being more satisfied, energized and productive!

Our focus in this shortcut is using the *SHIFT* process with your team. **I strongly recommend you teach the SHIFT steps to the team at a meeting so that folks aren't trying to learn the process during a big POW.** If you have been to one of my workshops or read *SHIFT to Professional Paradise*, you may be familiar with the *SHIFT* process. That's great! But don't stop reading now. This shortcut uses the same steps in a team environment and the review will be helpful.

What does *SHIFT* stand for?

 Stop and breathe.

 Harness harmful knee-jerk reactions.

 Identify and manage negative emotions.

 Find new options.

 Take one positive action.

I know from presenting this idea to thousands of people that many folks look at these five steps initially and think, "This doesn't look like rocket science, Vicki, it seems like common sense." Yes! I agree. **When team members are hit with a POW, they don't want rocket science – they want a simple shortcut to help them get to WOW as quickly and easily as possible.**

The *SHIFT* technique is proven. Healthcare leaders and employees across the country are already using it to be more engaged at work. It works for every position and level in the organization – individual contributor, leader and senior executive. It also works for individuals, teams, departments and entire organizations. It works for almost any POW you might experience. It just plain works!

The success of the process lies in the positive intention of using it and consistency of practice. The steps offer a concrete and productive way to talk about problems that arise. So often, leaders jump right to what to "do" to overcome a challenge. The *SHIFT* process focuses on the "human" part of the POW so that everyone is able to move past their frustration to implement the tactics to move forward. It provides a way to manage the negative knee-jerk reactions and feelings that often result from POWs. It opens the door to a more resilient and productive workforce – and isn't that exactly what you need? Let's look at each step individually.

Stop and breathe.

This simple step allows team members to pause and experience the benefits of deep breathing. Deep breathing increases the concentration of oxygen in the blood and releases endorphins that promote relaxation. This is exactly what people need when they've been hit with a POW. Fortunately, everyone has all of the equipment they need to execute this first step wherever they are – in the hallway, in a conference room, or in an office. Making the deep breath a conscious process slows down reactions and buys time. Quite often, POWs take us by surprise. This step gives everyone the time needed to collect themselves.

Harness harmful knee-jerk reactions.

A knee-jerk reaction is something that occurs automatically without thinking. Thankfully, we have grown accustomed to many helpful knee-jerk reactions, like pulling our hand away from a hot stove or flame. When team members have been hit with a POW, their knee-jerk reactions usually fall into the "fight or flight" category. In the days of cavemen, this knee-jerk reaction literally saved lives! However, in today's healthcare workplace, fight or flight isn't very helpful and can even cause bigger POWs.

Three common negative knee-jerk reactions to POWS are to pout, shout or lash out. In the heat of a POW, team members may not feel like they can harness these reactions, but with practice, they will be able to. Talking about them together speeds up this process. Negative responses only multiply the stress, anxiety and trouble created by the POW. Everyone benefits when we harness our negative knee-jerk reactions. When you talk about potential knee-jerk reactions with the team together, everyone realizes they aren't alone and can support each other in harnessing them.

*I*dentify and manage negative emotions.

The next step in the team *SHIFT* is to quickly identify the negative emotions that team members are experiencing and then proactively manage those emotions. Managing negative emotions is a natural part of life at work. You can help your team excel in this area by acknowledging challenging situations, letting people share their feelings, suggesting various coping mechanisms and encouraging them to help each other create more positive emotions.

The good news is that you don't have to have a degree in psychology to help others learn the steps for managing negative emotions. Common acute emotional management techniques include taking more than one deep breath, counting to 10, saying a prayer, taking a walk, etc. For more ideas on how to manage negative emotions, read *SHIFT to Professional Paradise.*

Just as importantly, team members need to manage emotions at the systemic level. Encourage employees to take care of themselves outside of work so that when they get hit with POWs at work, they are better able to manage the emotions in the heat of the moment. I've asked healthcare team members across the country what they do outside of work to manage their emotions at work. Common responses include exercise, spending time with family and friends, hobbies, community service, prayer and reading.

It's a shame that we don't share with our staff the healthy living lessons that we share with patients and their families. Too often, it is leaders who create more stress for employees or pressure them to work more hours and skip vacations. Why not promote a healthy lifestyle through your actions and support? Referrals to your employee assistance program are also helpful for employees suffering from excessive stress.

 *F*ind **new options.**

This step puts the team in a position to proactively deal with the POW rather than reactively deal with habitual knee-jerk reactions and negative emotions. When the group takes a few minutes to consider new options on how to deal with the POW, they move closer to WOW and closer to creating Professional Paradise – in spite of the POW. Having a choice provides a feeling of being in control, which most people appreciate. Being creative and thinking of a variety of options opens up possibilities that may have previously gone unnoticed. Encourage members of the team to tap into their individual strengths when coming up with solutions for managing the sting of the POW.

Encourage the team to find lots of fresh options. For the big POWs they encounter, brainstorm at least three to five new options. Try asking the team these three questions to spark some new ideas:

1. What have we done in the past when hit with a POW like this?

2. What would someone we admire do in a similar situation?

3. What would someone who is objective do to shift this POW to a WOW?

 Take one positive action.

Once the team has uncovered new options for managing the POW, the final step is to choose at least one that feels right for the situation, then take action! This is the action part of *SHIFT*. It takes what was merely positive thinking and moves it toward reality. Remember, thoughts alone rarely achieve anything. You must act if you want a better outcome.

The team may choose to implement more than one option, but one is the minimum needed to create a true *SHIFT*. Which option will produce the best results for managing the effects of the POW? Which one will create a win/win situation for those involved? Which one will get the team to WOW fastest or create the biggest WOW?

That's it! Those are the five steps to *SHIFT* any POW to a WOW. Using this technique with a group of employees (or your peers on a leadership team) can transform virtually any negative or unpleasant situation into one that's not only tolerable but also productive and beneficial.

Team Exercise
SHIFT Team POWs to WOWs

Every team gets hit with challenges – some more difficult than others. Using the *SHIFT* steps – deliberately and consistently – helps each individual and the collective team get to WOW much quicker. It's best to teach the team how to use the *SHIFT* steps when they aren't experiencing the negative consequences of a POW (at a team meeting, for example). Equip your team now so they will be prepared to *SHIFT* their POWs to WOWs. At the end of this exercise, team members will be able to:

✦ Review definition of POW and WOW;

✦ Describe the "why" behind shifting POW to WOW;

✦ Explain *SHIFT* steps and how a team can use them.

To save you time and make this easy, there are two options for facilitating this exercise:

1. Plug & Play – At your next team meeting, simply play a video I've already created and let me facilitate for you.

2. Plan & Present – Use the Leader's Guide in the BONUS TOOLS section to adapt the exercise to your needs and facilitate the meeting yourself.

You can access the video and Bonus Tools at
www.6ShortcutsToEngagement.com

Does *SHIFT* Actually Work?

Absolutely! Here's a real-life example that illustrates how one manager used the *SHIFT* process with her team. The case management department at a community hospital was going to be restructured due to staff turnover, budget constraints and regulatory changes. People's jobs were changing dramatically. They were facing a new reporting structure, moving to new offices and using new technology. Clearly, this was likely to be a huge POW for her team.

We called a team meeting and together we helped the team *SHIFT* this POW to a WOW so that everyone could continue to best serve the patients and their families. The manager gave an overview of the changes and shared that we would be using the *SHIFT* process (the team was familiar with the steps from previous training). Here's how it played out.

Stop and breathe. The manager asked the team to take a deep breath. Everyone did this together. Then she suggested that we take another one just for good measure – folks laughed.

Harness knee-jerk reactions. I asked the team to share what kinds of negative knee-jerk reactions people might display in response to a big change like this one and we recorded their answers on a flipchart. They started out slow – I gave a few examples, and then they responded with the following list: complain, pout, withhold information from each other; *complain; pout;* start looking for a job; bad-mouth the decision; *complain, pout,* form cliques; sabotage the effort, etc.

Identify and manage negative emotions. The manager asked the team how they were feeling about the change and she recorded those responses on a second flipchart. That list included the following emotions: fear, anger, frustration, feeling overwhelmed, uncertainty, worry, etc. We then talked about things people could do while at work (and at home) to effectively manage these emotions. Since this was a group of nurses and social workers, they had the knowledge to come up with a great list of ideas. These included creating an informal support network, increasing communication between peers, taking breaks, going for walks together, taking care of themselves outside of work, etc.

Find new options. We used the three questions to encourage the group to brainstorm new options for dealing with their negative reactions to the restructuring:

1. *What have you done in the past in a similar situation?* Some of these team members had worked at the hospital years ago when a similar change had taken place – they shared their ideas. A few folks had been through similar restructuring at other organizations and they shared what had helped to minimize the frustration during that transition.

2. *What would someone you admire do?* The group laughed about how as nurses and case managers they were frequently educating patients and family members about how to cope with change. Then they shared ideas about what admired "change-agents" had done.

3. *What would someone who is objective do?* In the weeks leading up to the meeting, the manager had done a great job of keeping the team informed about the change process, explaining the financial implications and sharing longer-term plans for growth at the hospital, which included this important department. Everyone agreed that when looking at the changes from these objective viewpoints, most of them made sense.

 Take one positive action. The manager facilitated a discussion where the group came up with a list of positive actions for coping with the POW. One item was a request for the manager to provide a "Monday Update" email with a review of the past week's changes and news so that everyone would feel informed, decreasing anxiety about unknowns. Another item dealt with how to communicate new contact information for team members because folks were worried about not being able to provide great service to their patients. The group also decided to meet on Fridays in the hospital cafeteria for an informal lunch so that everyone would feel connected and no one would feel left out.

The case management team left the meeting feeling more informed and in control. They had proven that they could manage this change more effectively by using the *SHIFT* process. Over the next few weeks, there were definitely bumps in the road, but overall, the transition went much more smoothly than people had anticipated. Now that's a WOW! These Chief Paradise Officers did the work and saw the benefits.

When to *SHIFT*

You might be wondering when to use the *SHIFT* steps with your team. You can use them "real-time" during a huddle or stand-up meeting whenever a POW pops up. You can use them at team meetings for predictable and perpetual POWs. You can also encourage employees to use the steps to solve individual POWs that they are experiencing, such as a difficult co-worker or customer.

I use *SHIFT* whenever something starts to create stress in my life – at work or at home, whether I've caused the problem or someone else has. You can use *SHIFT* to help the team cope with big, highly stressful events like layoffs or a tragic workplace event. And yet, you can also counsel the team to use it for everyday nuisances such as a printer breakdown, having to reschedule a meeting or an offhanded comment by a colleague.

Team members can use the process on their own or in small or large groups. Encourage employees to huddle up and use the *SHIFT* process together when they get hit with an external POW that threatens to cause trouble, such as malfunctioning technology, staff call-outs, a crisis like severe weather or a safety issue. Several department managers have reported success with this process as evidenced by their teams using the *SHIFT* process when the manager isn't even there. Someone close to the POW calls a quick team gathering and initiates the process. That's a WOW in and of itself!

The ultimate goal, of course, is to not only get to Professional Paradise, but to stay there permanently. To do that, you must model the *SHIFT* steps and remind your team that the one thing they can control about POWs is their response to them. Team members must create a habit of consistently *SHIFT*ing POWs to WOWs. The habitual responses we have all developed in response to POWs have to be eliminated and replaced with new, helpful habits that lead to WOWs. This is how *SHIFT* will help the team get to (and stay in) Professional Paradise.

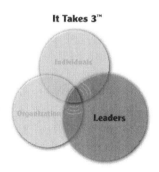

It Takes 3™

Shortcut #1: Embrace Employee Engagement

Shortcut #2: Create Connections

Shortcut #3: Shrink Team POWs

Shortcut #4: Grow Team WOWs

Shortcut #5: *SHIFT* Team POWs to WOWs

♦ Equip your team now so they will be prepared to *SHIFT* POWs to WOWs with five simple steps:

*S*top and breathe.

*H*arness harmful knee-jerk reactions.

*I*dentify and manage negative emotions.

*F*ind new options.

*T*ake one positive action.

Shortcut #6:
Measure and Monitor

Measuring and monitoring are hallmarks of healthcare. I remember learning about the importance of measurement in the assessment phase of the nursing process long ago in nursing school. It's logical that this focus on measurement would also be important when discussing team member engagement. I love this quote from George Bernard Shaw about measurement. *"The only man who behaved sensibly was my tailor; he took my measurement anew every time he saw me, while all the rest went on with their old measurements and expected them to fit me."* Like the tailor, we need to measure engagement on a regular basis so that we're not making decisions based on old measurements that don't fit where our team is today.

This shortcut is NOT about traditional measures of employee engagement such as annual or biannual organization-wide employee engagement surveys, NDNQI® surveys and "Pulse Check" surveys – all of which provide helpful information. I'm assuming that you, like most healthcare organizations I work with, have systems and processes in place for selecting highly competent survey vendors,

Beware of "Teaching to the Test"

I become concerned when I hear leaders talk about using terminology from their engagement survey so that employees will connect the dots between what leaders are doing to improve engagement and the survey itself (remember scripting for patient satisfaction?). The point of engagement surveys is to learn about perceptions, pinpoint areas for improvement and then make those improvements. It's natural to want to get "credit" for the actions you're taking to increase engagement, but this "vocabulary game" can be seen by team members as manipulative, which erodes trust.

When implementing strategies that improve engagement, we need to do it for the right reasons. For example, mandatory executive rounding is put in place so that executives are aware of what's happening in the organization and can make better leadership decisions. If survey responses about "being heard by executive leaders" happen to improve on the next survey, that's great. But remember, the end-goal is to positively impact engagement, not just get a good score. Be yourself and use your own words when talking with team members – your authenticity will pay off with higher scores.

conducting surveys, getting high levels of participation, reviewing results, cascading goals to staff and monitoring action plans. This is all worthwhile, and you should keep doing it.

Instead, we're going to look at aspects of measurement that are within your span of control as a leader. Our focus in this shortcut is "real-time" measuring and monitoring of engagement that will provide insights into your team's progress between annual/biannual surveys and support your efforts to sustain momentum so that everyone stays engaged. The idea is to layer an engagement component onto areas you're already measuring and monitoring so that it's realistic to add to your routine.

We've established that you are busy. I know if you are in a clinical area, you are inundated with things to measure: hand hygiene, HCAHPS, clinical indicators, other patient satisfaction measures, to name just a few. If you are in other areas, I'm sure you are measuring additional processes as well, such as usage statistics, waste, turnover, compensation benchmarks, training hours and infection rates. The point is that, most likely, you're already adept at measuring and monitoring, so this will be a breeze.

Here are four easy-to-implement methods for adding an employee engagement component to what you currently measure on a regular basis. Remember to think about "layering," not "starting from scratch."

✦ Environment Scan

The first method of measuring and monitoring engagement uses your senses. Anytime you are with members of your team, pay attention to the physical and emotional environment. How do people look? What does their body language tell you? What is the tone of the conversations? What's the "vibe," to use a very non-evidence-based term?

You don't need fancy charts and spreadsheets to conduct an environment scan. Simply be more aware, notice what is happening around you, and pay attention to the "feel" of the team. If you want to be more methodical about it – and I certainly recommend that – make brief notes in your calendar that document what you observe. This will help you spot trends and patterns over time.

✦ Employee Rounding

Since most of you are already doing some type of rounding with your team, this is the perfect place to add a measurement element for employee engagement. I described the Traffic Light Check-In process in Shortcut #2 (you might want to quickly review it now). **The Traffic Light Check-In is an especially powerful shortcut to engagement because it layers creating connections with team members and**

measuring and monitoring onto something you're already doing. It is an incredible optimization of your valuable time.

To add the measurement piece, simply keep track of raw data and root causes while you do your rounding. Informal tracking works fine, such as hash marks on a piece of paper for each person in the red, yellow and green zones. If people report being in the green or red zones, ask why and write that down as well. This allows you to track root causes for both high and low engagement and helps you identify what is working as well as what isn't. You can also delegate the Traffic Light Check-In to a team member (although you will lose the create-connections benefits).

Do you notice dips in engagement at the end of the month or during seasonal shifts in patient levels? What predictable, perpetual or preventable POWs are causing low engagement days? Are organizational or departmental changes leading to disengagement? The only way you will really be able to discover a causal explanation is by tracking the information and looking at trends.

Creative leaders add employee engagement to their PI/QI/ Lean Daily Management boards and measures. Making employee engagement measures visual promotes shared responsibility. For example, an IT manager could keep track of the responses to the Traffic Light Check-In with a Pareto Chart on the wall, along with other metrics that the team measures (e.g., help desk call response time and system down time). This not only highlights trends and patterns and themes, but also keeps employees focused on being satisfied, energized and productive. And when problems do arise that affect engagement, employees will be more likely to get involved in solving those problems. This shared measurement method promotes shared accountability.

Having a real-time method for tracking engagement gave her a distinctive edge, especially in times of rapid change or crisis management.

✦ One-on-One Meetings

When you hold one-on-one meetings with team members, as we discussed in Shortcut #2, you will hear anecdotal evidence of employees being satisfied, energized and productive. Adding the Satisfaction Snapshot on an occasional basis to the one-on-one meeting adds a more formal measurement piece. This questionnaire will help you gather anecdotal information about areas of engagement or disengagement so that you can focus on areas that need work and celebrate those areas that are working

 well. The Satisfaction Snapshot can be found in the BONUS TOOLS section of the book and can also be downloaded at www.6ShortcutsToEngagement.com.

I purposely didn't call this tool a "survey" because it is NOT meant to be a statistical tool but rather a great way to monitor engagement and start a conversation about engagement goals and current realities. The purpose is to measure each employee's internal and external motivators – what drives them to be satisfied, energized and productive – and their current satisfaction with those motivators.

The Snapshot uses one set of questions and asks the employee to rate two distinct variables related to engagement. The first variable is *how important* each element is to the employee. The second asks for feedback on *how satisfied* the employee is with each of those elements. The marriage of these two items is the single most informative thing you need to know to improve engagement. The "low-hanging fruit" for improving engagement are those areas that are very important and have low levels of satisfaction. The areas to celebrate are those that are very important and very satisfying.

The Snapshot also includes a few open-ended questions designed to consistently reinforce the message that each employee is accountable for his or her own engagement. Keep copies of each team member's snapshot and use them as a way to measure progress. You can also track responses from all team members and aggregate that information if you want to see overall trends.

In general, employees appreciate being asked their opinion about elements of work. Start with a manageable number of people and work your way through the staff from there. Just make certain you follow up with one-on-one conversations to listen, learn and brainstorm. The worst thing you can do is ask team members to complete the Snapshot and then do nothing with the information.

✦ Team Meetings

Team meetings are an incredible opportunity to leverage your engagement tactics:

> ✧ At the beginning of every team meeting, take two minutes to do a quick Traffic Light Check-In with the people in the room. You'll instantly have a feel for how engaged or disengaged team members are at that moment.

✧ During the meeting, scan (i.e., monitor) the environment to observe how team members are reacting to the information being presented. Do they perceive it as a POW or a WOW?

✧ If anything presented in the meeting is perceived as a POW, do a quick *SHIFT* to move people to a more positive mental state.

I hope you're starting to see how laying engagement activities onto the things you're already doing every day can have a dramatic positive impact with your team. There's one last element you can layer onto your team meetings: a measurement component.

Positive momentum is created when formal employee engagement surveys are completed and the results are shared. However, that momentum often decreases over time. Rather than having to wait months until the next survey comes out, gather real-time feedback on areas that have been identified as needing improvement to adjust your engagement approach. Use the following team exercise (or something you create on your own) to gauge progress since the last survey and facilitate a discussion about improvements.

Team Exercise
Engagement Survey Interim Feedback

The purpose of this exercise is to get real-time feedback on areas that have been identified from the most recent employee engagement survey. To make this team meeting measurement-focused, use informal tools like index cards to have folks anonymously share where things stand now. At the end of this exercise, team members will be able to:

✦ Rate their current satisfaction level with areas from the employee engagement survey;

✦ List who is responsible for each area;

✦ Create ideas for improvement.

 To save you time and make this easy, use the Leader's Guide in the BONUS TOOLS section to adapt the exercise to your needs and facilitate the meeting yourself.

You can access the video and Bonus Tools at
www.6ShortcutsToEngagement.com

Most organizations use data from annual or biannual employee engagement surveys as their only or primary source of measurement of employee engagement. While these surveys are certainly important, I would argue that they aren't especially helpful in guiding leaders in their daily jobs. The good news is that you can measure and monitor your team's engagement on a regular basis by adding a simple measurement component to your daily activities. **Real-time information allows you to make adjustments that will keep your employees satisfied, energized and productive, day in and day out.**

It Takes 3™

Shortcut #1: Embrace Employee Engagement

Shortcut #2: Create Connections

Shortcut #3: Shrink Team POWs

Shortcut #4: Grow Team WOWs

Shortcut #5: *SHIFT* Team POWs to WOWs

Shortcut #6: Measure and Monitor

✦ It's just as important to measure and monitor employee engagement as other healthcare metrics.

✦ Real-time measurement of engagement provides insights for keeping team members satisfied, energized and productive.

✦ Engagement components can be quickly and easily added to your daily activities through environment scans, rounding, one-on-one meetings and team meetings.

The Ultimate Goal – The Triple "Win"

Employee engagement is important for every organization in every industry. But it is especially crucial in healthcare where the work involves life-and-death consequences. The overarching goal of every healthcare organization is excellent patient care. Everyone says it a little differently, but when the rubber meets the road, that's why we're all here. The goal is to be of service to patients and to act as a conduit to the best possible health outcomes for all. A patient win is the BIG WIN!

Whether you lead a direct patient care area or a team that supports those on the frontline, your role is vitally important. You are thankfully leading the charge for providing this excellent care. Your organization's patients, their families and friends are glad that you invest your time and talent working to reach the goal of the patient win.

In order to achieve the patient win, the organization and the employees must also win. This is what I call the Triple Win in healthcare – achieving the best possible outcomes for patients, the organization and employees.

For an organization to be strong and healthy (i.e., "win") it must be financially stable. An organization in dire financial straits can't effectively serve patients. Financial stability involves being able to meet payroll, support infrastructure and promote growth. This is being threatened by decreasing inpatient volumes, the impact of government regulations and policies, and managed-care implementation. I trust that you and your executive leaders are laser-focused on this win.

The third win is what this book has been about: employee engagement. The employee win is actually the most critical win because it drives the other two. Employee engagement is the foundation for exceptional patient care and organizational financial stability. If we want to achieve the patient and organizational wins, then employees must win, too. And that means employee engagement must be equally as important as patient care and finances.

Improving employee engagement is the way
to accomplish everyone's goals.

In a do-more-with-less healthcare environment, now more than ever, your job as a healthcare leader is to focus on growing and sustaining employee engagement. As I shared in the beginning of this book, current studies indicate that 60 percent to 70 percent of healthcare employees are disengaged. Our mission must be to flip that scenario to one in which 60 percent to 70 percent of healthcare employees are actively engaged.

Just imagine the impact on patient care and financial stability
if together we could flip the stats!

The solution is to help team members find a true and lasting connection to their work that results in sustained internal motivation. Employees must embrace their role and become accountable for their own engagement. In other words, we have to help every team member find their own Professional Paradise.

The focus of this book has been what you can do as a leader to provide an engaging environment and help your team accept responsibility for their own engagement. If you are a senior leader, you also need to commit to working with the executive team to influence your organization's strategic focus on employee engagement. Remember, It Takes 3 – the organization, leaders and individuals – for sustainable engagement.

You've now discovered six shortcuts for growing employee engagement. In the BONUS TOOLS section, you'll find 12 quick, easy-to-use tools and four videos to support you moving forward. This is a great time to take a few minutes to prioritize how to get started. Please don't skip this step. If you do, you'll end up moving forward without a real plan, and your investment in reading this book will be minimized.

1. **Take the *Employee Engagement Checkup*** in the BONUS TOOLS section. Notice that the questions correlate to the six shortcuts.

2. **Tally your overall score** to determine how healthy you and your team are when it comes to engagement.

3. **Identify your biggest engagement challenges** by examining the scores pertaining to each shortcut. Which shortcuts did you score the lowest on? Write them down in the chart on the following page.

4. Determine your engagement treatment plan.
Flip back through the book and BONUS TOOLS to determine the shortcuts that will have the biggest impact on you and your team right now. Write those in the applicable space in the chart below. Then, prioritize which shortcut you will work on first.

5. Take action! Remember, you need to do the team exercise in the "It Takes 3" chapter titled, "*Whose Job Is It to Make You Happy at Work?*" first. It is the foundation for everything else. Then implement the shortcuts one at a time. Remember to layer the ideas onto activities you're already doing. Let team members process the information, implement change and create a new, positive habit before moving on to the next idea.

Priority	Biggest Engagement Challenges	Which Shortcut Do You Need?
1	Establish shared accountability	Whose Job Is It to Make You Happy at Work? Team Exercise

Keep your eyes on the final destination – The Triple Win – and know that It Takes 3 to achieve that goal. Commit to being the Chief Paradise Officer of your job and to helping your team do the same. When you embrace the idea that engagement is foundational and change your actions as a result, the outcomes will be rewarding, refreshing and revitalizing. You will have found Professional Paradise!

6 Shortcuts to Employee Engagement Executive Summary

✦ The challenges you're facing as a healthcare leader can be improved through optimized employee engagement. Increased employee engagement drives improved patient satisfaction, quality, safety, productivity and efficiency, as well as virtually every other metric that we track in healthcare.

✦ The It Takes 3 model focuses on shared responsibility for engagement:

It Takes 3™

Individuals

Organization   Leaders

1. An organization that deliberately and consistently supports employee engagement at the strategic level.

2. Leaders who regularly drive engagement at the tactical level.

3. Individuals who are accountable for engagement at a personal level.

✦ Executives and leaders talk about "employee engagement"… team members don't. Employees relate to the idea of being satisfied, energized and productive or Professional Paradise.

✦ Every person in the organization – from the frontlines to the C-suite – must become the Chief Paradise Officer of their job and "own" their personal engagement. Only when every team member chooses to be engaged and accepts responsibility for their own engagement can we achieve sustainable results.

✦ As a leader, you are responsible not only for the leadership aspect of engagement but also for role modeling engagement as an individual.

✦ You will get better results faster and with less effort when you layer employee engagement concepts onto the framework of your existing systems and processes. The 6 Shortcuts provide a fresh, realistic approach to engagement.

Shortcut #1: Embrace Employee Engagement

✧ Understand beliefs and mindsets.

✧ Create a shared vocabulary.

✧ Learn what gets people satisfied, energized and productive.

Shortcut #2: Create Connections

✧ Employees want and need more connection and communication.

✧ Use regular rounding to check in on engagement levels.

✧ Include engagement elements in team meetings.

✧ Conduct regular one-on-one meetings for high-impact results.

Shortcut #3: Shrink Team POWs

- ✧ Problems, challenges and obstacles – or POWs – can lead to disengagement in even the most engaging environments.
- ✧ Work with your team to identify the biggest POWs that affect them.
- ✧ Strategize ways to minimize the team POWs.
- ✧ Take action to shrink or eliminate them completely.

Shortcut #4: Grow Team WOWs

- ✧ Focusing on and celebrating successes – or WOWs – grows engagement.
- ✧ Help employees connect internally to what gets them satisfied, energized and productive.
- ✧ Proactively look for ways to grow WOWs for your team every day.

Shortcut #5: *SHIFT* Team POWs to WOWs

- ✧ Equip your team now so they will be prepared to *SHIFT* POWs to WOWs with five simple steps:

  *S*top and breathe.

  *H*arness harmful knee-jerk reactions.

  *I*dentify and manage negative emotions.

  *F*ind new options.

  *T*ake one positive action.

Shortcut #6: Measure and Monitor

- ✧ It's just as important to measure and monitor employee engagement as it is other healthcare metrics.

✧ Real-time measurement of engagement provides insights for keeping team members satisfied, energized and productive.

✧ Engagement components can be quickly and easily added to your daily activities through environment scans, rounding, one-on-one meetings and team meetings.

Bonus Tools, Tips & More Shortcuts

Bonus Tools, Tips & More Shortcuts

*All tools in this section can be accessed at
www.6ShortcutsToEngagement.com/BonusTools

Whose Job Is It to Make You Happy at Work?
Team Exercise

This exercise is important for getting buy-in around who is responsible for employee engagement. Asking for input from team members allows them to focus on their own beliefs and mindsets to form their own conclusions about engagement. This method works far better than telling employees what you want them to think and expecting them to agree.

At the end of this exercise, team members will be able to:

✦ Define employee engagement;

✦ Prioritize who is responsible for their engagement;

✦ Agree on key elements of creating a culture of engagement.

To save you time and make this easy, there are two options for facilitating this exercise:

1. Plug & Play – At your next team meeting, simply play a video I've already created and let me facilitate for you.

2. Plan & Present – Use the Leader's Guide below to adapt the exercise to your needs and facilitate the meeting yourself.

Both the video and Leader's Guide can be accessed at
www.6ShortcutsToEngagement.com/BonusTools

Materials: Index cards, flipchart paper, markers

Define employee engagement
✦ Share this easy-to-remember definition of employee engagement – when employees are satisfied, energized and productive.

Prioritize who is responsible for employee engagement.

◆ Give each team member an index card.
  ◇ Ask them to write "Myself," "My Leader," and "Organization/Executive Leaders" down the left side of the card.

	Rank (#1, #2, #3) Who Is Most Responsible for Your Engagement
Myself	
My Leader	
Organization/ Executive Leaders	

  ◇ Now ask them to rank (#1, #2, #3) who is most responsible for them being satisfied, energized and productive at work. For example, the one most responsible is ranked #1.
  ◇ Collect the cards and ask someone to tally the results while you continue with the next exercise.

Agree on key elements of creating a culture of engagement.

◆ Divide the staff into teams of three to four people.
  ◇ Ask each team to record on flipchart paper the things that positively influence their ability to be satisfied, energized and productive (i.e., compensation and benefits, teammates, personal goals, etc.).
  ◇ Allow 7 minutes for this part.

◆ Now ask the group to code the list according to who is responsible for each influencer.
  ◇ M = Myself
  ◇ L = My Leader
  ◇ O = Organization/Executive Leaders

✦ Ask groups to report their responses and make a master list of ideas for those that fall into these two categories: 1) Myself and 2) My Leader (these are the two groups within your direct control). NOTE: Be sure to collect the lists to evaluate the responses for the organization category for later review.

✦ Draw three circles (ex: It Takes 3 illustration shown in Shortcut #1) on a white board or flipchart paper and explain the diagram.

✦ Share the results of the index card exercise and ask for thoughts about the totals.

✦ Explain how each element (individuals, leaders, organization) contributes to employee engagement using specific examples from the list the group created.

✦ Add other things that both you and the organization are doing to promote engagement.

✦ Ask employees to discuss their contribution.

✦ Ask team members to find a partner and answer this question: "What is one thing I know I could do to be more engaged at work?"

✦ Ask for volunteers to share their responses.

Summarize

✦ Review the definition of employee engagement.

✦ Place the focus on what's within each individual's control.

✦ Commit to working on elements that are within your control.

✦ Thank everyone for his or her participation.

Would You Like to Work in Professional Paradise?
Team Exercise

Use this exercise during a team meeting to create a shared vocabulary for engagement with your team. If you already have common terminology that you use related to engagement, by all means use that.

At the end of this exercise, team members will be able to:

✦ Define employee engagement.

✦ Share examples of times at work when they are satisfied, energized and productive.

To save you time and make this easy, there are two options for facilitating this exercise:

1. Plug & Play – At your next team meeting, simply play a video I've already created and let me facilitate for you.

2. Plan & Present – Use the Leader's Guide below to adapt the exercise to your needs and facilitate the meeting yourself.

Both the video and Leader's Guide can be accessed at www.6ShortcutsToEngagement.com/BonusTools

Materials: Index cards

Define employee engagement

✦ Share this easy-to-remember definition of employee engagement – when employees are satisfied, energized and productive.

✦ Use Professional Paradise, Professional Prison and Professional Parole as a way to talk about varying levels of engagement and how they all interrelate.

✦ Introduce the idea of being the CPO – Chief Paradise Officer – of your job.

✦ Talk about the Chain Gang – giving it a name can help people realize if they are members.

Share examples of times at work when they are satisfied, energized and productive.

✦ Ask team members to think about what Professional Paradise means to them – when are they most satisfied, energized and productive?

✦ Hand out index cards.

✦ Invite team members to write down one or two examples of times when they have felt satisfied, energized and productive in the last week – there's no need to include a name.

✦ Collect the cards, redistribute them and ask each person to read what is on the card they received. (To increase interest, you can ask the team to guess who wrote it.)

Summarize

✦ Let team members know that you will be talking about this with them individually in more detail in the near future.

✦ Conclude the meeting by asking team members to actively look for and celebrate those times when they are satisfied, energized and productive each day.

 The Match Game

It's important to understand specifically what gets each employee satisfied, energized and productive and then match that to their daily job as much as possible. Discussing this with each team member provides a chance to talk about the shared responsibility for engagement and the employee's personal role. If you have regular one-on-one meetings, use that setting to bring up the conversation. If not, simply schedule a short get-together to talk it through.

Don't worry; you don't have to stop everything to get these get-togethers scheduled. Just put a sign-up sheet on your door with times you are available and let folks know that you want to meet with each of them. I know you are busy, so do what's realistic based on your schedule. Just don't put this off for too long because you'll end up spending time on engagement-related issues, whether you want to or not.

Ask the Question
Start by asking the same question asked at the team meeting: "*Give me a few examples of times when you've felt satisfied, energized and productive at work.*" It may take a few minutes for the employee to come up with something. Avoid filling in the silence and just let him or her think about it for a few minutes. You can provide personal examples or ask follow-up questions. "When do you feel time flying?" "When are you 'in the zone'?" "What part of work do you look forward to?"

Listen carefully and learn more specifically what gets and keeps each team member engaged and in Professional Paradise. You'll notice that some responses are internally driven and others are based on external experiences. Both are fine, although the goal is to be more internally motivated so you don't have to count on others to find

Professional Paradise. Remind the employees that they have the power to connect to these motivators every time they work simply by paying attention and noticing the "paradise" parts of their day. That's how each person creates his or her own Professional Paradise.

Make the Match

Keeping track of what gets each team member satisfied, energized and productive might seem daunting, but it's actually easier than you think.

On a white board (or pieces of flipchart paper) in your office, write "Professional Paradise" at the top. Then write down each team member's name. During your meetings discussing engagement, ask each person to write down one or two things (on the board next to their name) that gets them satisfied, energized and productive.

On a second white board entitled, "We Are Making a Difference" (or the name of your choice), post projects, work in progress, committees, learning opportunities, etc. Examples include: lean daily management teams, unit councils, IT implementation teams and new-employee orientation mentors.

When something new gets added to the We Are Making a Difference board, match team members based on what gets them satisfied, energized and productive. Also, ask employees to drop in periodically to see what's on the board and to let you know when something looks like a good match to them.

This is a great way to figure out whom to assign to which projects. You can look at the board and find the best match with someone who will be energized by the work. That's the Match Game in action!

The Traffic Light Check-In

This is a high-impact, easy-to-use tool to check in on levels of employee engagement when you are rounding with your team. It also allows you to gather real-time data and spot trends with respect to how engaged employees are. Read through this overview and figure out how to make it your own. This process needs to be comfortable and authentic, so adjust it to match your style.

✦ Announce in a team meeting that you will be asking employees to let you know how satisfied, energized and productive they are as you make your rounds. Explain that you will be using a traffic light as a metaphor. Describe the three levels of engagement using the colors red, yellow and green:

  ✧ Red: not satisfied, energized and productive (feeling stuck in Professional Prison)

  ✧ Yellow: somewhat satisfied, energized and productive (out on Professional Parole)

  ✧ Green: very satisfied, energized and productive (enjoying Professional Paradise!)

✦ The next time you're going to do rounding, get in the right frame of mind before you leave your office. Your job during rounding is to listen and learn. Avoid becoming rushed, defensive or frustrated.

✦ When visiting staff, tell them you're there for a "Traffic Light Check-In" and ask what color best reflects how satisfied, energized and productive they are feeling today. Be sure to follow up with questions that reinforce the idea that they are responsible for their own engagement.

✧ "I'm here for the Traffic Light Check-In – are you having a red, yellow or green day?"

✧ Follow with, "What are you doing to get to green?" (This question promotes personal responsibility for engagement.)

✧ "How can I support you?" (This shows your interest as a leader and coach.)

Listen thoughtfully. Don't worry about solving all of the problems and challenges right there on the spot. Oftentimes, team members simply want to be heard and they know that you can't make everything perfect. If you can't do anything at all about an issue, explain why and brainstorm creative ways to get around the roadblock (we will focus on this in the next Shortcut). For more complex issues that you need to be involved in fixing, make a note to follow up and ask the team member their ideas for improvement.

To add a measurement component, simply keep track of raw data and root causes while you do your rounding. Informal tracking works fine, such as hash marks on a piece of paper for each person in the red, yellow and green zones. If people report being in the green or red zones, ask why and write that down as well. This allows you to track root causes for both high and low engagement and helps you identify what is working, as well as what isn't. (Read more about measurement in Shortcut #6.)

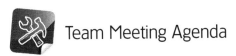

Team Meeting Agenda

Here's a sample agenda for a one-hour team meeting that creates connections. Please ask for staff input before the meeting and get others involved. If doing presentations energizes someone on your team, share the job of running the team meeting with him or her. Perhaps he or she can be the emcee!

Of course you'll want to add your own "flair" to keep things interesting. Use technology, such as teleconferencing, so employees who aren't working can participate or record the meeting for others to listen to afterward. Ask for help from your IT department if you aren't familiar with how technology can help you communicate virtually at team meetings.

1. **Reconnect with the vision and values:** A great way to dialogue about shared values and responsibilities is to connect them to positive work done by the team. Recognize individual team members or team efforts and connect the compliment to the vision. Ask others to share good news, too, and then relate it to the vision and values as well. For example... *"I want to recognize Bonnie, who demonstrated our STAR values when she went above and beyond to get the month-end report finished even with two team members out sick. Great job, Bonnie! Who else would like to recognize someone for showing off our STAR values?"*

2. **Share updates:** Share news from management meetings, including strategic initiatives, budget information, technology updates, etc. Your direct reports appreciate your candor and openness when it comes to keeping them informed, especially during challenging times. This is the time to dispel rumors and share important or complex information so that team members can ask questions. Please don't simply repeat items you've sent out in emails – people are likely to think that meeting (or reading your emails) is a waste of their time.

3. **Focus on Engagement:** Take 10-20 minutes at every team meeting to do an interactive exercise that focuses on engagement. (You can use the Match Game to find a willing facilitator whom you can delegate this to.) This is the perfect time to complete one of the team exercises from this book. The one in Shortcut #6 regarding your Engagement Survey Interim Feedback will help you with the measurement piece. There are other ideas at www.VickiHess.com – just click on "Free Resources."

4. **Take suggestions:** Open the floor for staff to share their ideas. Be clear that the topic is not "problems to solve" but "suggestions for improvement." You can use traditional brainstorming techniques, small-group discussions, or a pros-and-cons list to help determine any next steps. Get everyone involved.

5. **Gratitude and wrap-up:** Invite staff to share things about work that they are grateful for. This allows for positive reinforcement and public appreciation while ending on a good note.

One-on-One Meeting Tips, Sample Agenda & Grid

Here are some tips and techniques for effectively and efficiently conducting one-on-one meetings with each of your direct reports. Feel free to add your own elements to complement those included here.

Timing

Schedule the meeting regularly and in advance. Meeting monthly is ideal, but bimonthly or quarterly meetings will also work. Allow 20-30 minutes and block the time on your calendar with no interruptions. To make this easier, schedule three one-on-one meetings in a block of 90 minutes on your calendar. (This avoids the stop-and-start mentality that can be an energy zapper.) Allocate 20 minutes for each meeting with 10 minutes in-between to take notes and refocus for the next meeting. This way your mind is focused on creating connections, and the process goes more smoothly.

> **Special Note for Nurse Managers**
>
> Many nurse managers have more than 75 team members reporting directly to them across three shifts with 24/7 coverage. I can read your mind... "I can't possibly meet with folks monthly!" I understand. For you, I recommend two options.
>
> **Option 1:** Work with your "middle" layer of leaders (Clinical Coordinators, full-time Charge Nurses, Patient Care Coordinators, etc.) to teach them how to conduct monthly one-on-one meetings with their team members.
>
> **Option 2:** Meet with each team member quarterly. That breaks down to approximately two 90-minute time slots weekly for one-on-one meetings. This comes out to six people each week who get your undivided attention and time. This timing is a minimum frequency for one-on-one meetings to be effective.

Try this for several months. Initially it may seem like a lot, but over time you will see that it might just be the best use of 20 minutes when it comes to improving team member engagement. Be sure to flex your schedule so you can meet when folks are already working or are in the office for other meetings (all shifts). Asking someone to come in on a day off for a 20-minute meeting is de-motivating, and that's what we are trying to avoid.

Agenda

Managers use a variety of formats for one-on-one meetings. Here is a sample agenda that adds a specific layer of engagement to the meeting. Remember, this is a shortcut, so use what's working already and tweak it to directly make the connection to engagement.

1. What's New?

This simple question is a great way to start the meeting. Just ask and listen. Getting to know team members as individuals is the perfect way to build your relationship. Of course if you know about important life events that have occurred – upcoming milestones, vacations, continuing education, etc. – ask about those as well.

2. What's Working?

Start with the good news. Ask team members to share things that have been going well and then share your thoughts on progress since your last meeting. This is a great time for genuine praise. Ask about areas that were identified in the last Engagement Survey that you are working on to make sure that progress is being made.

Looking at what's working in the following three areas can be helpful:

✧ Performance (quality, productivity)

✧ People (compliments, team efforts)

✧ Projects (milestones, accomplishments)

Check in about the parts of their job that they identified as making them feel **satisfied, energized and productive** (you should have that posted on the board in your office from the Match Game). You can also use the Satisfaction Snapshot referenced in Shortcut #6 to learn more specifically what's important to a team member and his or her real-time satisfaction level. Ask how you can help the team member create more opportunities to do those things and ask how the team member plans to create more opportunities for him or herself. Focus on internal drivers of engagement (autonomy, self-sufficiency, gratitude, etc.) to promote shared accountability.

3. What Needs Work?

Ask for ideas and suggestions for improving the department or job. By challenging the employee to come up with solutions, you can make sure this isn't a gripe session. What are areas of development he or she seeks? Really listen so the employee feels that his or her opinion counts. This is a great time for owning challenges you have contributed to, sharing possible solutions or apologizing if warranted.

Looking at what's NOT working in the following three areas can be helpful as well:

- ✧ Performance (internal roadblocks, external barriers)
- ✧ People (inter- and intradepartmental challenges)
- ✧ Projects (conflicting priorities, missing tools or resources)

4. What's Next?

If any action items arise during the meeting, summarize and agree on who is responsible, the time frame and method of accountability. Do not feel like this is a "monkey exchange" where you take the proverbial monkey off the team member's back and put it on yours. Share responsibility for engagement moving forward.

I've created a One-on-One Meeting Grid to help you keep track of the agenda and what you talked about (with shared accountability) so that you don't have to spend time doing that. You can quickly and easily download a copy of the grid at www.6ShortcutsToEngagement.com/BonusTools.

One-on-One Meeting Grid

Name _____   Date _____

Agenda Item	Things You Will Follow Up On & the Deadline	Things Employee Will Follow Up On & the Deadline
What's New? ✦ Ask and listen ✦ Personal milestones ✦ Relax and be yourself! Connect		
What's Working? ✦ Performance (quality, productivity) ✦ People (compliments, team efforts) ✦ Projects (progress, accomplishments) ✦ Connect to what gets the employee satisfied, energized and productive.		
What's Not Working? ✦ Performance (internal and external barriers) ✦ People (inter- and intradepartmental challenges) ✦ Projects (conflicting priorities, missing tolls or resources)		
What's Next? ✦ Who is responsible for what's moving forward? ✦ Deadline dates? ✦ Items for next meeting?		

Tackle Team POWs
Team Exercise

Now that you've thought about some of the POWs that the team experiences, it's time to get their input as well with this easy exercise. When you complete this exercise about everyone's role in shrinking POWs, you are planting the seeds for team members to be the Chief Paradise Officer of their job. Consider it an investment in the individual accountability of your team and you will see vast returns in productivity, service, quality, etc., over time.

At the end of this exercise, team members will be able to:

✦ List and categorize common POWs that they experience.

✦ Take action to shrink the POWs.

To save you time and make this easy, there are two options for facilitating this exercise:

1. Plug & Play – At your next team meeting, simply play a video I've already created and let me facilitate for you.

2. Plan & Present – Use the Leader's Guide below to adapt the exercise to your needs and facilitate the meeting yourself.

Both the video and Leader's Guide can be accessed at
www.6ShortcutsToEngagement.com/BonusTools

Materials: Index cards, flipchart paper, markers

List and categorize common POWs that they experience.

✦ Define POW – something internal or external that feels like a heavy blow.

✦ Define internal and external POWs and share examples.

✦ Distribute at least 10 index cards to each person.

✦ Ask each person to make a list of POWs they regularly

experience (not on the worst day and not on the best day) and write one POW on each index card. It's very important that each team member do this on his/her own before you start a group discussion. You will get much more relevant data this way.

✦ Divide into groups of four or five.

✦ Ask team members to share their cards and put their POWs in categories that match each other's responses. For example, all POWs about difficult patients or internal customers go together; all POWs about technology go together, etc.

✦ Ask each small group to agree on their Top 3 most frustrating POWs.

✦ Ask each group to share their Top 3 while you write them down on a flipchart or white board. If a group mentions a POW that another group has already mentioned, put a check mark next to that POW to reflect the mention.

✦ Look at the combined list and, through group discussion, agree on the Top 5 most disengaging POWs.

✦ Define Predictable, Perpetual and Preventable POWs and share one example of each.

✦ As a team, identify which kind of POW the Top 5 are (Predictable, Perpetual or Preventable).

Take action to shrink the POWs.

✦ For POWs that are "owned" by others in the organization, brainstorm ideas for who needs to be involved and who will oversee the shrinking of the POW. Is this something that is created at the Organization/Executive Leader level or something that you as the leader can help with?

✦ The last step is to ask the group what they personally can do to shrink each POW or to manage their response to the POW.

Summarize

✦ We all experience POWs at work every day.

✦ Shrink those that are within your control.

✦ Work together with others outside your department to shrink bigger POWs.

The WOW Challenge
Team Exercise

In the shortcut about POWs, you spent time focusing on the challenges in your area. This team exercise focuses on the WOWs! The WOW Challenge is a contest that rewards individuals who uncover team WOWs on a regular basis.

At the end of this exercise, team members will be able to:

✦ List common Team WOWs they experience;

✦ Describe ways to grow more WOWs.

Materials: Inexpensive poker chips (like the kind you find at the dollar store); nine small prizes ($1-$3 each); three larger prizes ($5-$10 each). You can find inexpensive prizes at the dollar store or go to www.VickiHess.com and view the Products tab for prize ideas, such as WOW buttons, Professional Paradise pads, *28-Day Professional Paradise Diaries,* etc.).

List common Team WOWs they experience.

✦ Announce to the team that you are going to have a "WOW Challenge." Ask team members to be on the lookout for team WOWs, such as working together to meet a shared deadline or solve a problem.

✦ Everyone who brings you a list of five team WOWs will receive a chip (be liberal with your definition of a team WOW – the goal here is to get everyone focused on the positive aspects of work).

✦ At the end of a week, give prizes to the three people with the most chips.

Describe ways to grow more WOWs.

✦ Give a chip to anyone who comes up with a great idea on how to grow team WOWs, such as adding a moment for gratitude at a team huddle.

✦ Continue the contest for three weeks and, at the end, recognize the three people with the most overall chips. Provide a bigger prize (gift card, coupon to cafeteria, etc.) to reward and recognize these individuals as Chief Paradise Officers! If your team is made up of salaried employees, a great prize can be an extended break or extra time off. (Check with your supervisor or the HR department to make sure this is okay.)

Summarize

✦ Reinforce that the biggest rewards come for each person as they become more aware of the daily WOWs they experience.

✦ This practice is a great way to grow internal and external WOWs.

SHIFT Team POWs to WOWs
Team Exercise

Unfortunately, there will be times when POWs hit the team despite all of your best efforts. When the circumstances warrant a team approach, using the *SHIFT* steps – deliberately and consistently – helps each individual get to WOW much quicker. It's best to teach the team how to use the *SHIFT* steps when they aren't experiencing the negative consequences of a POW, so I recommend completing this exercise at a team meeting.

At the end of this exercise, team members will be able to:

◆ Review the definition of POW and WOW;

◆ Describe the "why" behind shifting POW to WOW;

◆ Explain *SHIFT* steps and how a team can use them.

To save you time and make this easy, there are two options for facilitating this exercise:

1. Plug & Play – At your next team meeting, simply play a video I've already created and let me facilitate for you.

2. Plan & Present – Use the Leader's Guide below to adapt the exercise to your needs and facilitate the meeting yourself.

Both the video and Leader's Guide can be accessed at
www.6ShortcutsToEngagement.com/BonusTools

Materials: White board or flipchart and markers

Review the definition of POW and WOW.

◆ POW – something internal or external that feels like a heavy blow.

◆ WOW – something internal or external that makes you feel satisfied, energized or productive.

Describe the "why" behind shifting POWs to WOWs.

✦ The *SHIFT* steps are a tool to manage your response to POWs that are out of our control.

Explain the *SHIFT* steps and how a team can use them.

SHIFT is an acronym for a series of steps that can be used to transform any POW to a WOW. It simplifies the process of changing ineffective, detrimental thought patterns and actions into positive, beneficial thought patterns, actions and habits. It works well with individuals or teams.

What does *SHIFT* stand for?

 Stop and breathe – Deep breathing promotes relaxation and gives people time to collect themselves when they've been hit with a POW.

 Harness knee-jerk reactions – Negative responses only multiply the stress, anxiety and trouble created by the POW.

 Identify and manage negative emotions – Acknowledge challenging situations, let people share their feelings, suggest various coping mechanisms, and encourage them to help each other create more positive emotions.

 Find new options – Proactively deal with the POW rather than reactively deal with habitual knee-jerk reactions and negative emotions; having a choice helps people feel in control. Ask three questions:

1. What have we done in the past when hit with a POW similar to this?

2. What would someone we admire do in a similar situation?

3. What would someone who is objective do to shift this POW to a WOW?

Take one positive action – Which option will produce the best results for managing the effects of the POW?

When a POW hits the team, anyone can take the initiative to gather the group and go through the steps together. This might be done in a quick huddle or in a longer, team-meeting setting. The bigger the POW, the more time you will need.

To download and print an 8.5" x 11" worksheet, go to www.ProfessionalParadise.com and click on *SolutionSHIFT Guide*.

Summarize

+ We all experience POWs at work every day.

+ Shrink those that are within your control.

+ Work together with others outside your department to shrink bigger POWs.

+ If you can't change the POW, change your response using the *SHIFT* steps – as a team or individually.

Satisfaction Snapshot

This questionnaire will help you gather anecdotal information. In doing this, you will be able to determine what's important for each individual on your team. You also will learn more about how your team members think things are going now. I purposely didn't call this a "survey" because the goal in using it is to gain insight into each employee's internal and external motivators. It is NOT meant to be a statistical tool.

✦ The questionnaire includes 22 statements that should be rated on a scale of 1 to 5 regarding how important each item is and how satisfied the employee is with that item in their job. The marriage of these two items is the single most informative thing you need to know to improve engagement. The "low-hanging fruit" for improving engagement are those areas that are very important and have low levels of satisfaction. The areas to celebrate are those that are very important and very satisfying.

✦ You'll notice that this is not an anonymous questionnaire. Hopefully you work in an environment of trust where people are comfortable sharing their opinions. If that's not the case, simply tell staff not to include their name. You won't be able to gather individual data, but you will be able to identify trends across the team.

✦ Make copies of the questionnaire and personally give it to each team member to fill out. (To download and print an 8.5" x 11" version, go to www.6ShortcutsToEngagement.com/BonusTools.) In general, employees appreciate being asked their opinion about elements of work, but some people are not crazy about filling out questionnaires. So you will need to make a personal connection and tell each person why this is important to you as a supervisor. Be forthright, request their assistance, and set up a deadline and time to meet to discuss the responses.

✦ When you meet to review their responses, be sure to also talk about their answers to the open-ended questions as well. Notice that the first question focuses on the employee's responsibility for engagement. Make sure this isn't a one-way conversation with you getting loaded up with things to do to make the employee happy at work. Keep asking what's within the employee's control as well.

✦ Keep copies of each team member's snapshot and use them as a way to measure progress. You can also track responses from all team members and aggregate that information if you want to see overall trends.

✦ Start with a manageable number of folks and work your way through the staff from there. The worst thing you can do is ask for completed questionnaires and then not follow up individually. Make a point to have one-on-one conversations to listen, learn and brainstorm. **You'll be glad you did!**

Satisfaction Snapshot

Name: _____ Date: _____

As you complete this questionnaire, please think of your job and your direct supervisor – not on the best day and not on the worst day. Put "*Most of the time...*" before each sentence to keep yourself on track.

Rate **HOW IMPORTANT** each item is and **HOW SATISFIED** you are with that item in your job.

5 = Very; 4 = Moderately; 3 = Neutral; 2 = Not Very; 1 = Not

	How important is...	How satisfied am I with...
1. Connecting what I do to the strategic direction of the organization?		
2. Receiving regular feedback and coaching on my performance?		
3. Being part of a strong team of co-workers?		
4. Being asked for my opinion on changes in our department?		
5. Utilizing my strengths in my job?		
6. Being part of a compelling shared vision?		
7. Understanding what is happening at the organizational level?		
8. My supervisor holding all staff members accountable?		
9. Attending regular staff meetings?		
10. Having opportunities to grow and develop?		
11. Working in a safe environment?		
12. Having input into my work schedule?		
13. Participating in annual performance appraisals?		
14. Having my supervisor spend time in my physical place of work?		
15. Having support when dealing with change?		
16. Having enough staff to get the work done?		
17. Receiving compliments on my work performance?		
18. Meeting regularly one-on-one with my supervisor?		
19. Having an environment of trust within our team/department?		
20. Utilizing a shared process for real-time problem solving?		
21. Achieving productive results at work?		
22. Feeling satisfied and energized about my job?		

One thing I could do to be more satisfied, energized and productive at work is...

One thing my supervisor could do to help me be more satisfied, energized and productive is...

Engagement Survey Interim Feedback
Team Exercise

Positive momentum is created when employee engagement surveys are completed and the results are shared. But often the momentum decreases over time. The purpose of this exercise is to get real-time feedback on areas needing improvement, as identified on the most recent employee engagement survey. To make this team meeting measurement focused, use informal tools (such as index cards) to have folks anonymously share where things stand now.

At the end of this exercise, team members will be able to:

✦ Rate their current satisfaction level with areas from the employee engagement survey;

✦ List who is responsible for each area;

✦ Create ideas for improvement.

Materials: Index cards, white board or flipchart with paper and markers

Rate their current satisfaction level with areas from the employee engagement survey.

✦ Before the meeting starts, on a white board or flipchart write six statements from the survey that were identified as needing improvement. (For example, *I have the opportunity to contribute to decisions that affect me,* or *I have the tools to do my job effectively.*)

✦ Below these statements, write the scale that will be used to rate these statements: SA = Strongly Agree; A = Agree; N = Neither agree nor disagree; D = Disagree; SD = Strongly Disagree.

✦ At the meeting, explain that as a follow-up to the most recently completed employee engagement survey, you are asking for feedback on how things are going in the areas the team agreed to work on.

✦ Hand out index cards.

✦ Ask employees to write the numbers 1-6 in a column. Then read each statement and ask them to rate that statement based on the scale. Give people time to think about their answer and then record it on the index card next to the applicable number.

✦ Collect the index cards and redistribute them randomly.

✦ Divide into groups of three to four people to tally up the responses and report the findings. As a group, identify the key areas that are going well, then celebrate for a few minutes.

List who is responsible for each area.

✦ Now spend time on the areas that need work by focusing on who "owns" each area – the Organization, Leader or Individual. Some areas that need work will be a shared responsibility. For example, a concern about not receiving enough praise and recognition might be shared between the manager who needs to consciously increase recognition for individuals and the team members who need to praise and recognize each other.

Create ideas for improvement.

✦ Review ideas from past meetings.

✦ Create new ideas for shrinking this POW (identifying the category of POW can be helpful in this process).

✦ Agree on the next steps and hold the team accountable.

Summarize

✦ This exercise offers a way to gauge progress on results from formal employee engagement surveys.

✦ Focus on what team members can control, and "own" what is in your control as a leader.

Employee Engagement Checkup

How healthy is your team when it comes to employee engagement?
Are you missing warning signs that a disengagement diagnosis is on the horizon?
What should your engagement treatment plan be moving forward?

It's time for your *Engagement Checkup* to find out!

Please think about a typical week as a leader – not your best week and not your worst – and then rate each statement using the scale below. Be honest and objective – if you aren't, the only person you'll be fooling is yourself.

Scale: 5) Always; 4) Often; 3) Sometimes; 2) Rarely; 1) Never

	Score
I embrace employee engagement as part of my strategic goals. (Shortcut #1)	
Team members accept responsibility for their own engagement. (Shortcut #1)	
I connect with every member of my team one on one. (Shortcut #2)	
Team members connect with what gets them satisfied, energized and productive. (Shortcut #2)	
I work to minimize challenges that my direct reports encounter. (Shortcut #3)	
Team members actively minimize daily challenges. (Shortcut #3)	
I celebrate good things with employees who report to me. (Shortcut #4)	
Team members create their own success moments regardless of what is happening around them. (Shortcut #4)	
I use a specific process to stay on track when hit with challenges. (Shortcut #5)	
Team members use a specific process to stay on track when they encounter challenges. (Shortcut #5)	
I measure employee engagement. (Shortcut #6)	
Team members measure their own engagement at work. (Shortcut #6)	
TOTAL	

Scoring:

12-24: Life support needed! Your risk factors for disengagement are too high. It's time to focus directly on employee engagement. You and your team need help now.

25-45: Watch for warning signs of poor engagement health (increased turnover, low morale, more complaints, etc). There's room for improvement. Focus on easy-to-implement, high-impact ideas to help you and your team get re-engaged.

46-60: Congratulations! Your team is in great shape and you have a healthy culture of engagement. Keep up the good habits and add a few ideas from this book to see even more positive outcomes.

Endnotes

[i] "When We're Feeling Better, They're Feeling Better: How Hospitals Can Impact Employee Behavior to Drive Better Care Outcomes." Towers Watson, towerswatson.com, 2012.

[ii] "Social Knows: Employee Engagement Statistics," by Elizabeth Lupfer. Web log post: *thesocialworkplace.com*. The Social Workplace, Aug. 8, 2011. Web. July 12, 2013.

[iii] "The Results Are In," by Don MacPherson. Web log post: *modernsurvey.com*. Modern Survey, March 29, 2013. Web. July 12, 2013.

[iv] "Engagement and Culture: Engaging Talent in Turbulent Times." Hewitt Associates, aon.com, 2009.

[v] "Motivating Employees: A Look Across Industries," Motivating Employees: A Look Across Industries webinar, Don MacPherson, Minneapolis, MN. June 13, 2013.

[vi] "Motivating Employees: A Look Across Industries," Motivating Employees: A Look Across Industries webinar, Don MacPherson, Minneapolis, MN. June 13, 2013.

[vii] "Motivating Employees: A Look Across Industries," Motivating Employees: A Look Across Industries webinar, Don MacPherson, Minneapolis, MN. June 13, 2013.

[viii] *State of Engagement: Unveiling Modern Survey's Latest U.S. Employee Research*. Rep. Modern Survey, Mar. 2013. www.ModernSurvey.com

[ix] *The Progress Principle: Using Small Wins to Ignite Joy, Engagement, and Creativity at Work*, by Amabile, Teresa, and Kramer, Steven Boston, MA: Harvard Business Review, 2011.

[x] "UCD: » Measuring Gratitude," by Dr. Robert Emmons, Emmons Lab, University of California-Davis. http://psychology.ucdavis.edu/Labs/emmons, Aug. 8, 2011. July 15, 2013.

About the Author

Vicki Hess, RN, MS, Certified Speaking Professional

A highly regarded speaker, author, facilitator and consultant, Vicki provides her clients with expertise in employee engagement as well as workforce and leadership development. With more than 30 years of hands-on business and healthcare experience, Vicki's purpose is to provide inspirational and evidence-based strategies for workplace engagement to change thinking and improve outcomes. She works with healthcare organizations and associations across the country to positively impact employee engagement through consulting, workshops, retreats and keynote presentations.

Vicki is one of about 250 women in the world to have earned the Certified Speaking Professional (CSP) designation...the speaking profession's international standard for platform skill. In 2013, she was voted a TOP 5 Healthcare Speaker by Speaking.com for the **third year in a row**. In 2012, she was one of the top 10 speakers in the overall category, along with such notables as Tony Alessandra and Brian Tracy.

Vicki began her work in nursing as a second career in the early '90s as a Staff Nurse. She was fortunate to join the Staff Development department of Sinai Hospital, an urban teaching hospital in Baltimore, Md., which eventually became part of a major health system, LifeBridge Health. Ultimately, she was responsible for the non-clinical training and development of 6,000 employees system-wide.

Vicki holds a BSN from the University of Florida and a Master's Degree in Human Resource Development from Towson University. She was an adjunct professor at Johns Hopkins University Graduate School of Business for five years.

In addition to this book, Vicki is the author of several others, including *SHIFT to Professional Paradise: 5 Steps to Less Stress, More Energy & Remarkable Results at Work* and *The Nurse Manager's Guide to Hiring, Firing & Inspiring* (Sigma Theta Tau International, April 2010). She has also written for *Hospital & Health Network*, *Becker's Hospital Review*, NurseTogether.com and the *Baltimore Business Journal*.

Need More Help in Engaging Your Employees?

Vicki Hess works with healthcare organizations nationwide through a variety of tactics to positively impact patient satisfaction, quality, safety, profitability, etc.

Here are ways that she can help:

1. Workshops and Retreats for Leaders & Staff

The quickest way to have a positive impact on employee engagement is to gather all of your leaders to hear the message together. Vicki's highly customized workshops meet you where you are and move forward from there. When leaders hear the message together, a shared vocabulary is created, which leads to lasting results. She offers follow-up to further reinforce the key ideas.

2. Consulting With Leaders & Team

Sometimes teams and their leaders need extra help with engagement challenges. When you see employee complaints, absenteeism and turnover increasing, it's time to intervene. Vicki uses a proven needs-assessment process, makes recommendations and piggybacks on what the team is already doing that's working to facilitate positive change. This process quickly leads to improved engagement that is sustained over time. Vicki offers a fresh and realistic approach to improving engagement in spite of all the challenges you and your team face.

3. Keynote Presentations

Invite author Vicki Hess to open or close your association or organization's next conference or meeting. Vicki's customized, high-energy, one-of-a-kind presentations are specifically designed to help audience members become more satisfied, energized and productive at work. Vicki uses a pre-conference assessment process that digs deeper into your specific needs. She takes time to talk to your stakeholders to understand their specific challenges.

4. Employee Engagement Resources

Find powerful tools that take the guesswork out of engagement for you and your team at www.VickiHess.com.

+ Sign up to receive Vicki's monthly newsletter, *SimpleSTEPS*, which includes actionable ideas for optimizing engagement.

+ Read Vicki's blog where she poses questions and shares her thoughts about the challenges and solutions for increasing engagement.

+ Download FREE resources for leaders and team members. Just click on the "Free Resources" tab.

+ Order copies of Vicki's other popular and helpful books: *SHIFT to Professional Paradise: 5 Steps to Less Stress, More Energy & Remarkable Results at Work* and the *28-Day Professional Paradise Diary*.

"*6 Shortcuts to Employee Engagement* is a must-read book that digs into a critical dilemma in healthcare that has been either dismissed or ignored for too long. Total, 100 percent employee engagement is what it's about, and it cannot be ignored or dismissed any longer or the healthcare industry is destined to fail in its mission of taking care of patients! Hess's book is destined to be quoted and used by all those who are committed to total engagement and personal accountability. I highly recommend this very significant piece of sheer enlightenment!"

> **Chuck Lauer**, Author, Writer, Advisor & Former Publisher and Editorial Director of *Modern Healthcare*

"We all have limited time and resources in an ever-changing healthcare world. Employees are our heartbeat. If you want a clear, concise roadmap to elevate the level of employee engagement and satisfaction in your workforce, *6 Shortcuts to Employee Engagement* is a must-read!"

> **Dorrie B. Rambo**, Chief Financial Officer, Elder Outreach

"*6 Shortcuts to Employee Engagement* provides a comprehensive and simple approach that includes real solutions for today's leaders. Many books offer great ideas, but Vicki provides actionable tools that a leader can begin to use immediately. Vicki has connected the dots between employee engagement and improved productivity and provides tools and resources to help today's business managers do more with less. Reading this book is like having Vicki right there with you as a personal coach helping tackle real challenges. An enjoyable and easy read with actionable tools and resources that can be used immediately."

> **Carolyn L. Candiello**, Vice President, Quality and Patient Safety, Greater Baltimore Medical Center

Find FREE Downloadable Tools at
www.6ShortcutsToEngagement.com/BonusTools

To bring Vicki to your organization, visit
www.VickiHess.com

32229679R00077

Made in the USA
Charleston, SC
12 August 2014